"With extraordinary clarity of vision, Dr. Budziszewski pierces the heart of today's most vexing questions, such as abortion, homosexuality, and moral relativism. *Ask Me Anything* strips away the misleading rhetoric and twisted logic that often surrounds these issues and shows students how the Bible's demanding moral standards reflect the careful design of a loving God who wants to give them abundant life."

—JEANNE HEFFERNAN
assistant professor of political science, Pepperdine University

Here's another treasure for today's postmodern collegians—a super companion to *How to Stay Christian in College.* Dr. Budziszewski combines divine wisdom, common sense, and brilliant reasoning in a gripping medium that draws one into the essential interaction between competing worldviews."

—DAVID C. NESS, PH.D.
ministry consultant to university faculty

"Whether you've been enjoying Dr. Budziszewski's columns for years or are a brand-new addict, you'll love *Ask Me Anything*. It's an impressive accomplishment when so much wisdom can be brought to bear—so many problems solved, so much confusion cleared up—in such entertaining bite-sized pieces."

—J. FRASER FIELD
executive officer, The Catholic Educator's Resource Center

"*Ask Me Anything* tackles all the tough questions from dating to faith to homosexuality in a biblical and practical manner. This should be required reading for any college student."

—KERBY ANDERSON
national director, Probe Ministries

TH1NK
™

Go Ahead:

TH1NK: *about God*
about life
about others

Faith isn't just an act; it's something you live—something huge and sometimes unimaginable. By getting into the real issues in your life, TH1NK books open opportunities to talk honestly about your faith, your relationship with God and others, as well as all the things life throws at you.

Don't let other people th1nk for you . . .

TH1NK for yourself.

ASK ME ANYTHING

PROVOCATIVE ANSWERS FOR COLLEGE STUDENTS

J. Budziszewski

TH1NK Books
an imprint of NavPress®

TH1NK
P.O. Box 35001
Colorado Springs, Colorado 80935

TH1NK is an imprint of NavPress.

TH1NK and the TH1NK logo are registered trademarks of NavPress. Absence of ® in connection with marks of
NavPress or other parties does not indicate an absence of registration of those marks.

ISBN 1-57683-650-9

Cover design by Arvid Wallen
Cover photo by Matt Wallen
Creative Team: Terry Behimer, Candice Watters, Arvid Wallen, Kathy Mosier, Glynese Northam

Budziszewski, J., 1952-
  Ask me anything : provocative answers for college students / J. Budziszewski.-- 1st ed.
    p. cm.
  Includes bibliographical references.
  ISBN 1-57683-650-9
  1. Christian college students--Religious life. 2. Christian college students--Conduct of life. I. Title.
  BV4531.3.B825 2004
  248.8'34--dc22
                                2004011619

Printed in Canada
1 2 3 4 5 6 7 8 9 10 / 08 07 06 05 04

NECESSARY

CONTENTS

ACKNOWLEDGMENTS   7

INTRODUCTION   9

GIRL AND GUY STUFF

  1. Courtship, Part 1: Who's on First?   13

  2. Courtship, Part 2: The Moves   19

  3. Sex at the Edge of Night   25

  4. Strange Arrangements, Part 1: Does It Matter
     Who You Live With?   33

  5. Strange Arrangements, Part 2: Does It Matter
     Who You Date?   39

  6. The Peter Pan Syndrome   45

  7. Girl and Guy Letters   51

FAITH ON CAMPUS STUFF

  8. If the Reformation's Over, Can We Dance?   71

  9. A Skeptical View of Christianity   79

 10. Why Should I Believe My Belief?   87

 11. The Word Wars   95

 12. The Big Story   101

 13. The Worship Mall   107

 14. Faith on Campus Letters   113

15. Can War Be Justified?   137

16. Homophobia, Part 1: Rage   143

17. Homophobia, Part 2: The Seeker   149

18. Hot Letters   157

NOTES   171

ABOUT THE AUTHOR   175

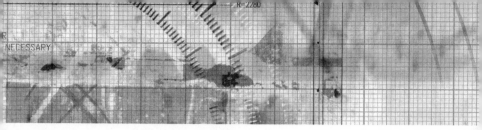

ACKNOWLEDGMENTS

My first thanks are to Sandra, without whom Theophilus would be mute. Gold there is and rubies in abundance, but lips that speak knowledge are a rare jewel.

I am grateful to all those who wrote to Theo, whether with questions or in anger, for they provided an opportunity to give back a tiny part of what has been given to me. Special thanks to those who wrote back, sometimes years later, to say that he had helped. They refreshed my spirit.

A monthly column in an online magazine is an odd thing for a professor to write. I owe the odd thought of doing it to the visionary founder of *Boundless* webzine, Candice Watters, who not only edited the column for the first three years but came back to edit this book.

This book is dedicated to all those I have never met who have become students of mine through Theophilus. May they become friends of the One from whose friendship he takes his name.

INTRODUCTION

*Therefore, since I myself have carefully investigated everything
from the beginning, it seemed good also to me to write an orderly
account for you, most excellent Theophilus.*

—LUKE 1:3

Dear readers:

Allow me to introduce my friend Professor M. E. Theophilus—
Theo to his wife, friends, and a few of his older students. Theophilus is
a college professor at Post-Everything University—not what you
would call Christian-friendly territory. The division in which he
teaches is called the School of Antinomianism, and he holds a position
there called the Chair of Pre-Modern Studies.

Theophilus got his position by a fluke. When he was hired, he was
a very different person than he is today. In fact, he was an atheist, and
it was only afterward that he became a Christian. As you might guess,
that changed the school's feelings quite a bit. Some of his colleagues
would love to get rid of him. They wish now that they hadn't awarded
him the PMS Chair. Lucky for him, he's tenured.

Students seem to be in his office all the time, confiding in him and
seeking his advice. As a college professor myself, I can tell you that this
is far from common. My students don't talk with *me* like that. Five years
ago, I began publishing some of Theo's conversations in a student magazine called *Boundless*. It's online; maybe you've seen it at www.bound-
less.org. One thing led to another. Soon the published conversations
were getting thousands of visitors, and mail began pouring in. As you
can see from the table of contents, this book contains a fair sample of
both his conversations and his letters.

I've called these dialogues Theo's "conversations." Are they word-for-word transcripts? Some parts are, but to make them suitable for publication I've had to take liberties. You can think of them as fiction in the service of real life. A lot of readers also ask if Theo and I are the same person. Let me set that notion to rest. As anyone who knows both of us can tell you, he's much cooler. I knew you'd want to know more about him, so the other day I passed on a few questions. Here's how our conversation went:

> *Budziszewski: What does the name M. E. Theophilus mean, and where does it come from?*
>
> *Theophilus: Luke addressed his New Testament writings to someone named Theophilus. The name means "Lover of God." An early bishop named Theophilus was also known for enlightening the Goths — sort of what yours truly does, don't you think? But I don't know how my family got the name.*
>
> *Budziszewski: You've only explained the Theophilus part. What about your initials, M. E.? I've always called you just Theo.*
>
> *Theophilus: Are you asking about my first and middle names? Those were my father's idea. He happened to be reading Luke 1:3 when my mother announced that she was pregnant. Ha, ha, Dad.*
>
> *Budziszewski: Then what do your students call you?*
>
> *Theophilus: "Perfesser."*

That's enough from me. I hope you like my friend.

Blessings,
The Author

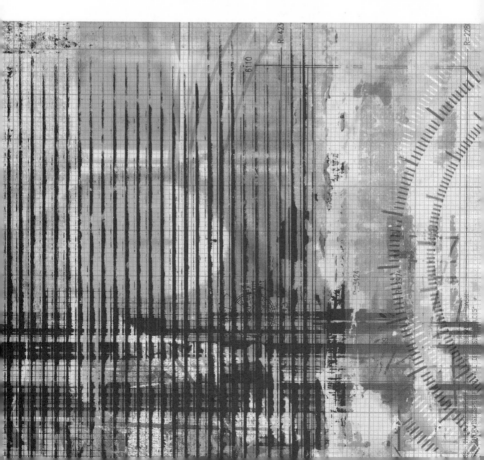

GIRL AND GUY STUFF

COURTSHIP, PART 1: WHO'S ON FIRST?

WHY IS IT SO HARD FOR MEN AND WOMEN TO UNDERSTAND EACH OTHER?

It was only a little past eleven. The Union was almost empty. Expecting a quiet lunch, I chose a table where I could look out the window at the Quad. No sooner had I set down my tray than a familiar face materialized. "Expecting someone, Prof?" It was Mark Manasseh.

"Not at all. Pull up a chair." He sat down with a plate of something I didn't recognize. "What's that? Some kind of taco?"

"Haven't you ever had a gyro?" he asked. "It's like a Greek taco. Gyros have been around for a long time."

I shook my head. "Food has changed."

"Food's not the only thing that's changed," he said and lapsed into a moody silence. He chewed meditatively.

"So what else has changed?" I asked.

"Huh?"

"You said food's not the only thing that's changed. What else has changed?"

"Oh. The rules. They're always changing them on you in the middle of the game. I can't tell who's on first anymore."

"Who's 'they'? Has the Faculty Senate changed the graduation requirements again?"

"No. Actually I was thinking of a girl." He played with his gyro and then looked up. "I guess I'm not being very clear."

"Clear enough—girl changes terms of relationship, guy confused. You don't have to explain."

"Maybe I should. You and I've talked about this kind of thing once before, and I could use the perspective of an, um, older person. Do you mind?"

I shook my head. "I have time. Being so old, you know."

"I only meant—"

I laughed. "I know what you meant. Go ahead."

"There's this girl, Molly. She's a friend. But that's it—just a friend. You know, we talk and do things together. But I talk and do things with *all* my friends."

"Do you talk and do things with them the same way you talk and do things with Molly?"

"Not exactly. She's a *close* friend." He paused. "But *just* a close friend."

I smiled. "Just very close."

"Right."

"And a girl."

"Right."

"When you talk and do things with her, are other people included?"

"Sometimes."

"Uh-huh."

"But I do things *just* with other friends too. Like I told her."

"Like you told her? How did the subject come up?"

"I'm still trying to figure that out."

"Suppose you tell me what happened."

"Well, we were hungry, so we were having a pizza together at Molto Alimento."

"Just because you were hungry."

"Why does there have to be another reason? Can't friends eat a pizza?"

"Sure."

"Anyway, we were almost done when she said something about how we've known each other for almost two years. I said yes. She said we've had a lot of fun together. I said yes. And then she said some other stuff . . . I don't remember what—you can't listen to everything a girl says or it would wear you out. I must have said yes to that, too, which was probably a mistake. Next thing I knew, she was talking about how a girl needs a commitment or something. I guess it took a few minutes for what she was saying to sink in, and I asked, 'What do you mean?' And she said, 'Commitment' and spelled the word. And I said, 'It's not like we've been dating or anything.' And she said, 'What do you call it when we've been seeing each other exclusively for two years?' And I said, 'What do you mean exclusively? I do things together with lots of other people.' And she said, 'Not with other girls you don't.' And I said, 'Girls and guys both.' And she said, 'What girls?' And I said I couldn't think of any and she asked me why I was holding back and I said I didn't know what she was talking about and then all of a sudden she was crying and she left the table and the waiter looked at me like I was dog meat and I couldn't find her so I went home. And I keep trying to phone her but she won't return my calls and it's all I can . . . I mean, I . . . well . . ." He looked embarrassed and took a deep breath. "So that's why I say she changed the rules."

"From what to what?"

"What?"

"What did she change them from, and what did she change them to?"

"From friendship rules to dating rules."

"But that's not exactly what she said, is it?"

"What do you mean?"

"You quoted her as asking something like, 'What do you call what we've been doing?' So she thinks you're the one who's trying to change the rules."

"But I *never* said we were dating!"

"But weren't you?"

"Don't I have to *think* it's a date for it to be a date?"

"Do you have to think a car is a car for it to be a car?"

"This isn't like that."

"Mark, when two people of opposite sex enjoy a social activity, it's called a date."

"But it wasn't *romantic.*"

"Not all dates are romantic, but any date is potentially romantic. That's why steady dating produces expectations, especially among girls. Life is short. Why should they waste their time dating guys who aren't serious?"

"We were never romantic."

"She thought you were."

"Yeah, well, I guess that's true."

"And are you so sure that it makes no difference to you that Molly is a girl? Would you worry like that if some guy wouldn't return your calls?"

"But she didn't say we were dating either. Not before. Once some-one asked if we were dating, and she answered before I even had a chance. She just laughed and said, 'Oh, no, we're just friends.' See? She *did* change the rules on me."

I sighed. "Mark, these days neither girls nor guys seem to want to admit that their dates are dates. But they have different reasons for not wanting to, and those reasons kick in on different occasions."

"What are you calling reasons? Start with girls."

"I think one common reason girls today don't call dates 'dates' is that guys today think 'date' means 'sex.' The idea of dating as courtship has almost disappeared."

"I don't pressure girls for sex."

"Does *she* know that?"

"She ought to. She knows I'm a Christian."

"I'm sure she knows that sexual intercourse outside of marriage is contrary to Christian principles. But a lot of so-called Christian guys *do* pressure girls sexually. How does she know that you won't?"

"I haven't pressured her *yet*, have I?"

"But you say you aren't dating, remember?"

"Oh. Well, yeah."

"She might think that one reason you haven't pressured her for sex is that up until now, she's gone along with the myth that you aren't dating."

"Maybe," he admitted.

"There's another reason."

"What is it?"

"Girls these days don't often call dates 'dates' because guys these days are so afraid of commitment. You won't say *that* one doesn't apply to you." Mark shifted uncomfortably in his chair. "You see, the girl may feel that the only way the guy will ever court her is if he doesn't have to admit that it's courtship."

"All right, I see your point. What do you say are the guy reasons?"

"We've already covered the first one," I said. "Girls are right — guys these days *are* afraid of commitment. It's part of their fear of growing up. And there's another reason: fear of failure."

"Fear of failure?"

"If you're 'just friends' and she says no to pizza, it's no big deal. But if you ask her on a pizza date and she says no, it's humiliating. To relieve the pressure, guys don't call dates 'dates.' That's related to another girl reason. Most girls don't *want* to humiliate guys, so if the guy doesn't call it a date, they go along with him."

"Stop. You're bringing back memories of junior high school."

"That's just it. Some guys never quite get past that stage."

"Are there any other guy reasons?"

"There's one more, but we've covered that one too."

"We have?"

"Sure. You mentioned it yourself."

"When?"

"Right at the beginning of the conversation. You said that the rules of relationships have changed and that you can't even tell who's on first anymore."

"It's true."

"Of course it is. Pressure for sex, fear of commitment, fear of failure—all these things have changed the rules of relationships. Add to these things the feeling that men and women are adversaries, and things look pretty grim. No wonder guys aren't willing to call dates 'dates.' They don't know what they might be getting into."

"Right!"

"The problem is that not calling dates 'dates' doesn't work either."

"Why not?"

"Think of your dinner with Molly."

"Oh." Mark thought for a moment. "So does *anything* work? What *are* the moves of courtship?"

COURTSHIP, PART 2: THE MOVES

NOT WHAT YOU THOUGHT THEY WERE.

Mark had been asking me about the "moves" of courtship. "The first moves are all in your head," I said, "and here's the first one: When you're enjoying a social activity with a girl, admit to yourself that it's inherently unlike a social activity with a guy friend. Call it what it is: a date."

"That makes it sound like it might lead to something," he grumbled.

"It *might* lead to something. That's the point. Dating generates expectations. The problem in our time isn't that it generates expectations; it ought to generate them. The problem is that too often it generates either wrong expectations or conflicting ones."

"What do you mean by that?"

"By what?"

"Wrong or conflicting expectations."

"An example of a wrong expectation is when the guy thinks he's entitled to sex. The sexual powers are too powerful to play around with outside marriage."

"I see *that* well enough. What about the conflicting ones?"

"For instance when the guy views the girl just as someone to have fun with, while the girl views the guy as someone she might be interested in marrying." I smiled wryly. "And I have to tell you, in a case like that, my sympathies are with the girl."

"Why?"

"Her biological clock ticks a lot faster than yours. From a purely physical point of view, you can father a child at almost any point in your life, but she has to have children while she's young. So it makes sense for her to view every date in terms of possible marriage — and it's childish and selfish for you to expect her not to."

He grimaced. "So from your point of view, the whole purpose of dating is for the girl to find a suitable marriage partner."

"No. For *both* of them to find a suitable marriage partner."

"Don't put any pressure on me or anything, Prof."

I laughed. "You call *that* pressure? I could put a lot more on you than that."

"Like what?"

"Like saying that you shouldn't date anyone you wouldn't consider marrying."

"Hey, wait," Mark said. "You're going pretty fast. That's not in the Bible, is it?"

I smiled. "No. Do you think that lets you off the hook?"

"Doesn't it? After all, we're Christians."

"Nope. When certain Corinthians threw in Paul's face their slogan that everything not forbidden is permissible, he replied, 'but not everything is beneficial.'[1] Thinking like a Christian means a lot more than doing what the Bible says; it also means thinking like the Bible thinks — even about things the Bible doesn't mention. That includes having respect for human nature as God designed it, like the difference between your biological clock and the girl's. It also includes realism about temptations."

"Well, okay, I guess I see that. But what if the girl *knows* I'm not interested in marrying her?"

"How do you know she knows that?"

"Because she says so. Why are you laughing?"

"Sorry. I happened to remember what my wife said about that to one of our nephews the other day. Her advice was that if you're dating a girl and she says she understands that you're not interested in marrying her, don't believe her."

Mark was scandalized. "You mean I should expect girls to *lie?*"

"No, no. Well, yes, they do sometimes, but no more than guys do, and that's not what I mean. It's just that if a girl says she understands a thing like that, she doesn't understand herself any better than the guy does."

"I don't get it."

"Have you forgotten already? Think of Molly, Mark, think of Molly."

He winced. "I get it."

"Any more questions?"

"Lots. What about this? You say that I shouldn't even date anyone I wouldn't consider marrying. But what if I'm not interested in getting married *at all*?"

"Are you not interested in getting married at all?"

"I don't know. I haven't thought about it much."

"Then start thinking now."

"Why? I don't *have* to get married, do I?"

"No. But there's a good reason and a bad reason to avoid marriage, and the matter isn't just up to you."

"What do you mean by that?"

"Some people—especially guys—avoid marriage because they're too selfish to get married. Actually, marriage and family are God's ways of breaking us *out* of our selfishness. So that's the bad reason."

He raised an eyebrow. "What's the good reason?"

"Jesus said that a few people are set aside by God for an unmarried way of life for the sake of the kingdom of heaven.[2] Paul talked about this too.[3] But Jesus made it clear that the single life is difficult. Those who are called to it should follow it; those who aren't shouldn't try. So it isn't just a matter of going your own way. In fact, it's the opposite of going your own way."

"So if, say, I was called by God to singleness—"

"Then common sense—*creational* common sense, the common sense about human nature that I called 'thinking like the Bible thinks'—says you shouldn't date at all."

"Because I'd be tempted?"

"Yes, that's one reason. And also because it would be cruel to arouse expectations of possible marriage that wouldn't be right to fulfill."

Mark blew his breath out through his mouth. "I don't actually think I'm called to a permanent single life."

"Maybe not. Let's suppose you're not. What then?"

"Then it's okay to date. As long as I date only girls I might consider marrying."

"Right. Any thoughts about what sorts of girls they might be?"

"Um . . . compatible girls?"

"Naturally, but what else do you need to know about them?"

"That they share my faith in Christ?"

"Right, that's a scriptural absolute, and I'm sure you can see why. What else?"

"That they're . . . hmm . . . mature? Of good character?"

"Good. Go on."

"That's all I can think of."

"In the Creation story, God blessed our first parents and then told them to be fruitful. Good thing for you and me that they obeyed that better than His commandment about the tree."

"You mean I should be looking forward to having kids? So I guess I shouldn't date a girl unless she would make a good mother too."

"Right. Just like she shouldn't date you unless you'd make a good father."

"Me being a father—that idea's a little hard for me to wrap my mind around, Professor Theophilus."

I smiled. "It's easier to do it than to envision it. We were designed for it."

"Do you have kids?"

"Several. Anything else you find it hard to wrap your mind around?"

Mark thought for a moment. "Yeah. One more thing."

"What is it?"

"Suppose I *did* decide I was interested—in marrying someone. I mean if she was . . . still . . . interested too."

"Go on."

"Suppose she *was* all those things—and I *did* feel something for her—though I'm not sure exactly what."

"That's hard for us males to sort out."

"Why is that?"

"I don't know. I have a theory, though. Want to hear it?"

"Yes."

"There's a part of the brain that communicates between the sensitive, emotional side and the rational, analytical side. It's said to be smaller in men than in women."

"So?"

"So my theory is that we men feel all the same emotions that women do, but we just don't notice."

Mark gaped at me for a second or two and then burst out laughing. "Are you serious?"

I grinned. "Only half serious. But you were saying?"

"Oh, yeah. Suppose I asked . . . this girl . . . to marry me . . . and she said yes. What then?"

"I'd say, 'Congratulations.'"

"That's not what I mean. I mean, what are the moves for *engagement?*"

"I'd say the moves for engagement take care of themselves. Except for one thing."

"What's that?"

"When two people know they're going to be married soon, they begin letting their guard down. Actually, this is one of the most important times to keep their guard *up.*"

"You mean sexually?"

"Of course. For example, they may have every intention of

remaining chaste but spend every waking moment alone together. That's a formula for disaster because being alone with the beloved is *supposed* to be arousing; that's how God made us. So they need to spend their alone time where there are other people within view." I paused. "But aren't you getting a little ahead of yourself, Mark? We were talking about dating. You haven't even decided whether you *want* to marry Molly."

Mark startled, then gave me a sheepish look. "Oh, yeah. I forgot."

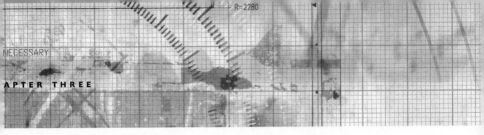

SEX AT THE EDGE OF NIGHT

WHAT IS SEX FOR, ANYWAY? DON'T LAUGH.

Don and I had just taken chairs at the Edge of Night. "Whatcha want?" asked the waitress.

"Espresso," I said.

"Pizza," said Don. "Sixteen-inch, double pepperoni, double grease."

She turned her gimlet eye back to me. "Y'want that espresso triple, double, or wimpy?"

"Wimpy," I answered. "Thanks." She slouched away.

"Wimpy?" said Don.

"Double grease?" I answered. We laughed. Don is always eating. A full eight inches taller than I am, he weighs at least thirty pounds less. You can draw your own conclusions.

"Um, can we talk now, Prof?" On the walk across campus he'd been telling me his problem with his housemate's girlfriend.

"Let's see," I said. "She came on to you; you didn't give in, but— how did you put it?—the experience raised some questions in your mind. What questions?"

"Well . . ." Don reddens easily, and he reddened now. "It's not that I'm . . ." Pause. "I mean, I know God intends sex for marriage, but . . ." Pause. "She's awfully good-looking, and I couldn't help wondering . . ." Dead stop.

"Wondering what it would . . ." I prompted. Not that I wanted to answer that particular question.

"No! I mean, yes, I did wonder that. But it's not my question."

"What's your question?"

"Why *did* God reserve sex for marriage? There must be reasons, but it would help a healthy guy a whole lot to know what they are."

I laughed. "I suppose it would."

"I'm not trying to second-guess Him or anything. I know He's right. Understanding would just make it *easier,* you know?"

"Sure," I replied. "I don't have the whole answer, Don. But I'll answer the best I can." He blew out his breath in relief.

Just at that moment, Don's buddy Wen came up — good fellow, but noisy. "Hey, Prof. Hey, Don. Whatcha talking about?"

"Professor T's just giving me the good line," said Don. "Right, Prof?"

"About what?" Wen asked.

I could tell Don didn't want to tell him, but he'd boxed himself in. "If you must know, sex."

"No kidding!" he exclaimed, grinning. He turned toward a group at the other end of the room. "Theophilus is talking about sex!" he yelled. Before we knew it, eight or nine guys were dragging chairs to our table. A few were with girls; I recognized Mary. Crimson, Don was cradling his head in his hands. His pizza arrived, and half of it vanished in a flurry of reaching hands. "We're talking about Don's sex life, right?" Wen asked. Lifting his head, Don shot me a look of appeal.

"No," I said, "about the philosophy of sex." Don looked grateful. "I was about to say something about why sex is reserved for married people."

"Your exotic reputation precedes you, Professor Theophilus. Enlighten us!" This from a fellow with glasses.

"Are all of you really serious?"

"Yes!" they chorused. I smiled wryly and shook my head. This was a little out of my previous experience.

"Okay," I said. "I don't have much time, so let's set limits. First, I'll discuss this issue only. Second, I'll only cover the Christian view, which is my own. Third, I'll only lay out the basics. Fair?" They agreed.

"But Professor T"—it was the glasses guy, the one who had called me 'exotic'—"isn't it obvious what you'll tell us? You'll harp about pregnancy and sexually transmitted diseases, then tell us the only way to keep safe is to wait for marriage."

A short fellow across from him interrupted. "Those seem like good reasons to *me*." A half-dozen voices broke out, some in agreement, some in dispute.

"Hold on," I broke in. "You're missing the point. Anyone listening would think that if only condoms worked perfectly, then extramarital sex would be all right."

"Wouldn't it?" asked Shorty. Everyone laughed.

"What's wrong with that picture?" I asked.

"Well, they *don't* work perfectly," suggested a red-haired young man. "You could drive a truck through the pores in latex rubber."

"But you could imagine technology that did work perfectly. Try again."

Don spoke up. "Is it that even with perfect technology, you couldn't get people to use it?"

"No. You could imagine an even better technology that worked independently of their wills."

Glasses interrupted. "Are you getting at the idea that our list of bad consequences is incomplete?"

"That was my thought," said a blonde young woman seated next to him. "Even a perfect shield against pregnancy and disease would leave consequences like jealousy and mistrust untouched."

"But you could imagine a system of drugs and conditioning that would eliminate those consequences too."

"Like *Brave New World*," said Mary.

"Cool," said the red-haired fellow. "I read that in my English class. Aldous Huxley. Pneu*maaaaaaaa*tic." A few guys smirked.

"*Not* cool," said a tall girl. "The people in Huxley's paradise are loathsome. They don't understand the *point* of sex."

"And what is its point?" I asked.

"I don't know—but I know they don't have a clue."

"Come on, group," I urged. "A question is on the table. What is the point of sex?"

"The point?" asked Wen.

"The point! What is it *for*? What is its *purpose*?"

"That's obvious," he said. "Pleasure."

"No," I said. "Pleasure is great, but it comes as a by-product of doing things that are more important than pleasure. What happens when you pursue it for its own sake?"

"It disappears," said the tall girl. "My sorority sister is doing it more and more but enjoying it less and less."

"That's called 'empty' sex," I said. "If pleasure isn't the purpose, what else might the purpose be?"

"Love?" asked Mary.

"Depends on what you mean."

"You know, romantic feelings."

"If it's feelings we're talking about, we're in the same blind alley that we were with pleasure. Feelings are by-products. They don't make sense as goals. Besides, promiscuity destroys romance."

"How can you say that?" asked Shorty.

"Let the women answer," I said. "Women, how *romantic* is it to stand buck-naked in front of a man who hasn't given his life to you?"

Mary looked down. "Not very," she said.

"Besides," I went on, "love is not a feeling."

"Not a feeling?" asked the tall girl. "What else could it be?"

"Love is a commitment of the will to the true good of the other person. Otherwise, how could people getting married promise to love each other? You can't promise to have a feeling."

"That's why you need divorce," said Glasses.

"No, it's why marriage has to be based on something else," I replied.

"If love is a commitment of the will, what does sex have to do with it?" he pressed.

"Sexual union takes each spouse out of the Self for the sake of the Other."

"How?"

"Think. What is the *biological* purpose of sex?"

"That's obvious," said the blonde girl. "Having babies."

"Right. What are some other biological functions?"

"Eating!"

"Digestion!"

"Growth!"

"Good answers," I said. "Now pay attention. How many bodies does it take for you to do those things?"

"One," came the reply.

"And how many does it take to procreate?"

"Two."

"Can you think of any other function that your body can't perform on its own?"

"No."

"Then do you see how sex is special? In every other biological function, husband and wife are separate organisms; for procreation, they become one. Conjugal union is a true merging. They become a one-flesh unity. And I don't mean just flesh."

Mary cut in. "What do you mean, not just flesh?"

"I'm giving the Christian view, right? Now think. In the Christian view, if this is how we function, it's because this is how we were designed to function—by God. Do you follow me?"

"Yes, but—"

"Hold on. Now if God designed us to work this way, *He must have finished the job.*"

"What do you mean?" asked the tall girl.

"He wouldn't have stopped with the design of our bodies."

"What else is there?" asked Wen.

"Emotions?" she suggested.

"Emotions, and a lot of other things besides. We're designed for wholeness. You see, in sexual self-giving, the hearts and minds and spirits of the husband and wife *cooperate* with their bodies. They are united not just in their bodily dimension, but in every dimension. This unity also helps prepare them to be parents, and the hope of children joins them in solidarity with every past and future generation. That takes them out of the Self too."

"But you just admitted that love involves emotions," said Mary. "Didn't you say that love is not a feeling?"

"I said that love can't be *defined* as a feeling; I didn't say it doesn't *involve* feelings and all the other things. Of course it does."

The red-haired guy spoke up. "You've missed something, Professor T. If it's 'all the other things' that people want, then they can enjoy them now and settle down to a commitment later."

"You think so?" I answered. I snagged the waitress as she slumped past the table. "Miss, do you have some tape by any chance? I need something sticky." She produced a roll of silver-gray duct tape, slapped it on the table, and drooped off.

Don was amazed. "How'd you know she'd have that?"

"In a place like this they use duct tape for everything," I said. "What do you think is holding the cash register together?" Heads turned. "Now, Red," I said, "give me your arm."

"My what?"

"Your arm. Roll up your sleeve." He gave me a funny look but obeyed. Everyone watched intently. "Nice and hairy—good." I tore off a six-inch piece of duct tape and showed it to him. "Tell this tape, 'Don't stick.'"

"Don't stick, tape!"

"Let's see whether it obeys." I pressed it down on his arm, then counted, "One, two, three!" and ripped it off.

"*Hey!*" he gasped. Everyone laughed.

"Hmm. Let's try it again." Rip! "Better that time?"

He grimaced. "A little. How many times are you going to do that?"

"As many as it takes for the tape to obey." We did it five or six more times. Each time the tape was a little less sticky. "It seems that the tape has finally obeyed," I said. "Now tell it to stick."

"Stick, tape!" said Red. I pressed the tape on his arm. It fell off. I pressed harder. It fell off again.

"Do you get it?" I asked. "Your sexuality is like that too. The first time you use it, you're going to stick to whoever it touches. Sex can't help sticking; that's what it's *for.*"

"So if you rip yourself loose—" said Glasses.

"Then there's going to be damage. Something in both of your hearts will tear. Not only that, but when you do get loose, your sexuality won't be as sticky as it was before. What happens when you pull it loose from one person after another?"

"Eventually it won't stick anymore," said the tall girl.

"Right. Your sexual partners will seem like strangers; you just won't feel anything. You will have destroyed your capacity for intimacy. So there's your answer, Red. You can't have 'all the other things' now and commitment later."

"But how do you know if you have a commitment?" he asked.

"Easy," I said. "If you're married, you've got one. If you're not married, you don't." Dead silence ensued. I took advantage of it to look at my watch. "But I'm out of time. My wife is expecting me."

"Wait!" cried Don.

"*You can't leave now!*" cried the tall girl.

"You're not finished!" cried Mary.

"I want to argue!" cried Glasses.

"Argue during office hours." I smiled—and escaped. As I left the Edge of Night, I glanced over my shoulder. Shorty was pounding the table. The blonde girl was shaking her head. Wen, Mary, and four others were all talking at once.

A successful evening, I thought. Except for one thing.

I never did get my espresso.

STRANGE ARRANGEMENTS, PART 1: DOES IT MATTER WHO YOU LIVE WITH?

ONE OF THOSE NO-BRAINERS THAT PEOPLE FIND HARD TO FIGURE OUT.

I must have jumped when Chad spoke because he asked, "Did I startle you, Professor Theophilus?"

"Yes," I confessed. "Usually I hear people coming. You just shimmered in, like Jeeves."

"Who's Jeebes?"

"Never mind. Are you looking for someone?" He'd glanced over his shoulder.

"Yes, Sarah and Mary were supposed to be right behind me." At that moment they materialized.

Sarah smiled. Mary burrowed in her backpack, and with a shower of number two pencils, she extracted something and handed it to me. "Yours." I'd wondered what had become of that coffee mug.

"I'm glad to see you all," I said, "but I was just going out for a bite."

"Have it with us," urged Sarah.

I asked, "Is there a special occasion?" We left my office and began walking to the Edge of Night.

"Not exactly," said Mary, "but we need to pick your brain about living with nonChristians."

"Why do you need to pick my brain?"

"My fault," Chad said. "See, Professor Theophilus, I feel that part of my job here on earth is to make friends with people of different religions so that I can bring them into Christ's kingdom."

"I don't see the problem."

"Just wait," said Mary. "He's crazy." Mary was a new Christian, and her comments were a little snarky sometimes.

"Well," said Chad, "my old roommate moved out. I need a new one, so I'm planning to share the rent with this person I met who follows a different religion." Mary rolled her eyes.

"How different?"

"Real different." He told me what it was. I could feel my pupils dilating.

"Told you," said Mary.

When we arrived at the cafe, Chad asked the waitress for four cheeseburgers with fries and drinks. He had to call her back so the rest of us could order too. Sarah resumed the story. "See, Professor, we all belong to the same prayer group. So when Chad told us what he has in mind, Mary said he was—"

"Crazy," chirped Mary.

"And I thought so too. So we talked and talked, but we couldn't convince him. Finally we thought of getting an outside opinion."

"That's you," said Chad. "I promised Mary and Sarah that if you thought like they did, I'd give up the idea."

They looked at me expectantly. I took a meditative sip of water.

"Aren't you going to answer?" asked Mary. She looked sidelong at Chad. "How is he going to feel when it's his roommate's turn to cook and he finds eye of newt in his soup?"

"They don't do that stuff," said Chad. "They're just very interested in spiritual things."

"Spiritual!" she scoffed. "Which spirits?"

"Chad," I said finally, "I wouldn't worry much about eye of newt. But I do get the impression that you don't know much about your would-be roommate's worldview and moral outlook."

"Well, not yet."

"You see, the problem isn't just that your prospective roommate's religion is strange; difficulties would arise even if this person had no particular religion at all. Either way, you can't expect the behavior you could expect from a committed Christian."

"I figured that with a little tolerance, we could work our problems out."

"By itself, an agreement to be tolerant gets you nowhere."

"Why?"

"Well, tolerance doesn't mean tolerating everything, does it? It means tolerating tolerable things. To decide which frustrations are tolerable and which aren't, don't you need a moral framework?"

"I guess so."

"There's the rub. People think tolerance will enable them to get along even if they have different moral frameworks. The problem is that if your roommate's moral framework is radically different from yours, then your roommate's view of the tolerable may also be radically different from yours."

"How do you mean, Professor T?"

"Isn't it obvious?" asked Mary. "Before I was a Christian, I lived for a while with this Christian girl. She expected me to be tolerant of her friends coming over for things like prayer and Bible study, which I considered disgusting. To keep from hearing them pray, I'd turn up my music so loud they couldn't even hear themselves. She said I was intolerant because I insulted her friends and made her feel like a stranger in her own home."

"Then she was right," said Chad. "You *were* intolerant."

"The way I saw it, *she* was the intolerant one. It was one thing after another. She didn't want to hear my obscene music, she asked me to take down the Crispy Fried Jesus poster I'd put up in the kitchen, and she got mad the day I covered her bumpers with lesbian stickers as a gag. Get it? She was intolerant of my music, my decorating, and my sense of humor."

"Couldn't you negotiate?"

"Sure, but I'd always win."

"Why?"

"Because I held all the cards. Like Professor T said, we had different moral frameworks. When we disagreed about what was tolerable, her rule was 'Love your enemies' and mine was 'Get even.'"

"That's so extreme," said Chad. "It's hard to imagine anything like that happening in my case. My future roommate seems so . . . well . . . so nice."

Chuckling, I leaned back to flag the waitress for an espresso. Chad looked puzzled. "Why did you laugh just now?"

"I'm sorry. That word always reminds me of an old family story."

"What word? What story?" he asked.

"*Nice*," I answered. "You said your friend was *nice*. When my Uncle Millard finished serving time and they finally let him out, the first thing he said to Aunt Martha was, 'You know, you meet some of the *nicest* people in prison.' I'm sure he did too."

This time they all laughed. It broke the tension. "Okay, Prof, I'm almost convinced," said Chad, trying to look serious but failing. "But are you saying my whole idea is wrong?"

"What do you mean by your 'whole idea'?"

"Deliberately seeking out a nonChristian roommate. Suppose we *did* get along. Would you still think a nonChristian roommate was a bad idea?"

"Tell me again why you think it's so important to have one."

"You know, to have an influence. To win someone for Christ."

"Like I said, *crazy*," said Mary.

"What if *you'd* never had any Christian friends?" he retorted.

"It's not *friendship* you're talking about."

"Mary makes a good point," I interrupted. "In some ways, living together is much closer than being friends. Suppose you do get along. Suppose you do have an influence. How do you know that your roommate won't have a greater influence on *you*?"

"Hey! Is *that* all you think of my faith?"

"I have great respect for your faith. And, in most respects, for your maturity. But is it your faith speaking or your pride?"

"How could it be proud to want to evangelize someone?"

"Chad, forgive me for saying so, but you're still being formed. We all are. You can have lots of nonChristian friends, but your closest comrades should be your brothers and sisters in faith."

"Don't you think I can resist peer pressure?"

"Why exhaust yourself resisting peer pressure? Just get the right peers!"

Even Sarah seemed scandalized this time. "What?"

"I said, get the right peers!"

"I don't understand," said Mary.

"God didn't make us to be immune to the influence of other human beings," I explained. "He gave us social natures. The way to resist bad pressures isn't to pretend that you're made of steel. You resist bad pressures by putting yourself in the path of good ones. So, as I said, you need the right peers."

"Who are you calling my *right peers*?" asked Chad.

"Your right peers are your partners in Christ, the people with whom you share the household of God."

"So I can go ahead and evangelize my nonbelieving friends, but I shouldn't . . . I shouldn't put myself in an isolation chamber with them." He sighed.

"Still not convinced?"

"No, I'm convinced all right. It's just that she was already planning to move in, and I don't look forward to phoning and telling her it's off."

"Excuse me," I said. "Did you say *her*? The person you were planning to room with is a *woman*?"

"Didn't I mention that?" asked Chad. He shifted uncomfortably. "It's not like I'd have been sleeping with her or anything."

"That was one of the issues we argued about before we brought you in on the discussion, Professor T," said Sarah.

"Yeah," said Mary.

"See, I was trying to convince Chad that his living with someone who didn't know the Lord was a lot more serious than my just dating one," said Sarah.

"Suddenly this conversation seems to have speeded up," I said. "Did you just say that you're *dating* a nonbeliever?"

Chad perked up. Sarah reddened.

"She's crazy too," said Mary.

"Maybe we should order dessert," I suggested. "I don't think we're quite finished with this conversation."

STRANGE ARRANGEMENTS, PART 2: DOES IT MATTER WHO YOU DATE?

CHAD TURNS THE TABLES ON SARAH.

"Chad—" I stopped and rubbed my eyes. "Chad, about the girl you were going to share an apartment with—" *How do you explain the obvious?* "Look, I'm glad you're not going through with the idea. And I understand that you weren't planning to sleep with her. We don't have to spend time on it. But just in case you get a bright idea like that again, let me ask you, exactly how were you planning to turn off human nature?"

"What do you mean?"

"Perhaps you hadn't noticed, but opposites attract."

"I'm not attracted to her *that* way, Professor T."

I shook my head. "I hear this sort of thing all the time. A girl spends the afternoon with a guy, but it's 'not a date.' A guy has a special friend who's a girl, but she's 'not a girlfriend.' A girl and a guy are planning to live together, but he's 'not attracted to her *that* way.' We live in one of the most sex-obsessed societies in history, yet people try to tell me they don't have genders. I'm not buying it."

"But I'm *really not* attracted to her that way."

I turned to Mary and Sarah, who were enjoying Chad's discomfort immensely. "This girl Chad was going to share the rent with—is she pretty?"

"Hey! No fair!" Chad protested.

Mary just laughed.

"I don't know about *pretty,*" Sarah said cattily, "but she wears her skirt up to *here* and her blouse—"

That was all Chad could stand. "Okay, okay, okay! All right!"

"All right, what?" she asked.

"All right, you win. I wasn't being straight with myself. So lay off me. Besides," he added craftily, "I thought we were going to talk about the games *you've* been playing with yourself."

Sarah's smile evaporated, and her color, which had been fading for several minutes, began to heighten. "I don't know what you mean."

"He's talking about the guy you're going out with. The one who—"

"I *know* what he *means*, Mary."

Mary looked confused. "I thought you just said you didn't."

"We *were* going to talk about missionary dating," I reminded them.

"What's missionary dating?" That was Mary.

"Going out with someone under the pretext of evangelizing him."

"It's not a pretext," Sarah protested. "I really do want to evangelize him."

"Fine, but I'll stick to my description. There's always an element of self-deception in such relationships."

"Why do you say that?"

"I know," said Mary, "because if you want to convert the guy, convert the guy. What's stopping you? To convert him, you don't have to date him too. There must be some other reason."

"I don't have to date him to evangelize him, but if I'm dating him he's a lot more likely to listen."

"In that case, I sure would hate to be the guy," said Chad.

"Why?" Sarah bristled. "Do I have cooties or something?"

"No, but look at it from his point of view. Here's this poor chump thinking you like him, and all the while you're just using your sex appeal to trick him into church."

Mary piped in. "Either that or he's on to you, and he goes to church with you just so that—"

"But I'm *not* dating him just to get him into church."

"Why else, then?"

"Because I like him, okay? He's nice and fun to be with."

"Could you marry him?" I asked.

"Could I—what did you say?"

"Could you honestly ask Christ to bless a marriage between you and this fellow?"

"No-o."

Mary cut in. "Doesn't the Bible say somewhere that Christians should marry only other Christians?"

"Yes. Second letter to the Corinthians. Chapter six, last five verses."

"But I'm not planning to *marry* him. I'm only dating him."

"Dating is *about* marriage, Sarah. It's a search for a suitable marriage partner."

Sarah was appalled. "Are you telling me that I can't date anyone I can't marry?"

"That's exactly what I'm telling you."

"Isn't there such a thing as 'just friends'?"

"That was Chad's mistake—pretending that friends don't have genders."

She glanced at him. "But it's not like I'm in *love* with this guy."

"How do you know you won't *fall* in love with him?"

"Why should I think that will happen?"

"Don't you spend a lot of time with him?"

"Yes."

"How else do you think people fall in love?"

"But it doesn't *always* happen, right? I've dated lots of guys without falling in love with them."

"Okay, but what's better—to date only people it would be all right to marry, or to date people it wouldn't be all right to marry and just hope that you don't fall in love with them?"

"God wouldn't *let* me fall in love with—no, that's pretty stupid," said Sarah.

"Yeah, dumb," said Mary.

"Well, I guess I'll just *plan* not to fall in love with him."

"It would be nice if it worked that way, but it doesn't. That's not how we're designed."

"I'm emotionally mature. I can plan not to fall in love with someone."

"Sure you can. The way you plan not to fall in love with him is not to date him or spend time alone with him."

Mary interrupted. "Can you plan *to* fall in love with someone?"

"That's ridiculous," said Sarah.

"I sort of think it's what you're doing," said Mary.

"How can you say that?"

"When someone stands in front of a bus, I say she's planning to get run over."

Hastily, I cut in. "I do think you can plan to fall in love with some-one—not necessarily with a particular person, but with a particular kind of person."

"You mean like 'red hair, good-looking, likes modern jazz?'" asked Mary.

"No, I mean like 'shares my faith, would make a good husband, good with kids.'"

"How do you plan to fall in love with that kind of person?"

"You seek out and spend time with that kind of person, and you don't date the other kinds."

"But Professor T," said Sarah, "what if you just can't find that kind of person?"

"Then either you're looking in the wrong places," I said, "or else—"

"What are those places?"

"It isn't a mystery where to find Christians, is it? Either you're looking in the wrong places or else, secretly, you don't *want* to find that kind of person."

"What do you mean, 'secretly'?"

"I mean that people deceive themselves about their motives—and not just about dating. People plan all sorts of things they don't admit to themselves."

Chad asked, "Like what?"

"Planning to change their opinions, planning to get pregnant, planning to lose their virginity, planning to fall out of love with their wives—"

"I don't see how you could do those things without knowing it. How could you *plan* to change your opinions?"

"By associating only with people who hold the opposite opinions. Haven't you ever seen that happen?"

"Well, yeah. And I guess I do see how you can plan to lose your virginity."

"Sure. By putting yourself in the way of unnecessary temptations."

"But I still don't see how you can plan to get pregnant."

Mary rolled her eyes. "I'll explain it to you later."

"Do that," said Chad. "And I don't see how you can plan to fall out of love with your wife either."

"That's because you're not married yet," I said. "There are lots of ways. For instance, you might hire a beautiful assistant and take her with you on business trips."

Mary broke in. "And you might plan to fall *into* love with a guy by—"

"Never mind, Mary," said Sarah. "I can complete that sentence: by dating him."

Mary whacked her spoon on the table like a gavel. "Point carried! Conversation over! We can all go home!"

No one moved. Mary looked from one to the other. "What's the matter? Don't we all agree now? When you said, 'by dating him,' I thought you meant you get it now."

"Yeah. I get it now." Danger signal. Sarah never says, "Yeah."

"You couldn't marry him," said Mary.

"No."

"So you shouldn't date him."

"No."

"So you stop."

Sarah didn't reply right away. "That's the part I have to think about."

"Didn't we just *do* that?" demanded Mary.

"I know what I *should* do. I just have to think about whether I'm going to do it."

"If you know what you should do, how can you *not* do it?"

"I don't know! Okay? Let's not talk about it anymore."

Chad and I exchanged looks. "C'mon, Sarah," he said. "I'll walk you home."

They rose and moved away. Mary was almost frantic. "Professor Theophilus, Sarah was the one who converted me! Isn't she supposed to be further along than me? Isn't Jesus going to *do* something?"

I watched Chad and Sarah as they walked across the floor of the Edge of Night. "Maybe He already is," I said.

THE PETER PAN SYNDROME

FORTUNATELY, THERE IS A CURE.

As we left campus to catch a bite of lunch, Zack stopped at a pastel green building the locals call Guacamole Memorial. It's a private dorm, the largest in the student ghetto. He glanced at his Mickey Mouse watch. "D'you mind if we turn in here first, Prof? I forgot something."

"Would you like me to wait outside?"

"No, you can come in."

All in all I wished I hadn't; faculty could hardly be more conspicuous than in a place like this. Besides, it was coed, and as we passed girls in various stages of dress, I felt as though I were visiting a house of ill repute. Zack noticed my uneasiness and laughed. "After a while you get used to it, Professor T."

"I don't see how."

"There are two theories about that. One is that with all these girls living on the same floor you do, you start feeling like they're sisters. Incest taboo, you know?"

"What's the other theory?"

"Well, there's a lot of incest."

A few paces farther was his door. Turning the key, he said, "C'mon in. Don't step on the skateboard. I'll be just a sec."

My eyes scanned the room. On the bed was a water gun version of an AK-47 assault rifle; next to it lay a pile of comic books. On the desk perched a video game console, obscured by five or six Transformers and a Slinky. From the ceiling hung a model of a Star Wars craft—I think it was the Millennium Falcon. On the floor, a business textbook was opened to the section on Bayesian analysis; alongside it, a copy of

Horton Hears a Who was opened to the section where Horton is vindicated. A couple of limp mylar balloons were attached by laces to a pair of sour athletic shoes. Zack thrust his arm into a pile of clothes, thrashed around, and pulled out a leather wallet. "That's lucky," he said. "I was worried that the washing machine might have hurt it. Let's go." By prearrangement, we headed for the Edge of Night. He ordered a fried egg sandwich; I called for my usual Reuben. No sooner had we given thanks than he got down to business. "The reason I invited you to lunch, Professor Theophilus, was to ask your opinion about something."

"Go ahead."

"What's wrong with me?"

I studied him. "What makes you think there's something wrong with you?"

"Lots of things. For one, next semester I graduate, and I've just been admitted to the MA program in my field."

"Do you call that bad?"

"It is if you don't need an MA."

"But, Zack, if you don't need one—"

"Then why am I planning on getting one? That's just it. I don't know."

"I see."

"Here's another thing. There's this girl, Julie. You know her."

"Yes. Nice girl."

"Well, I'm crazy in love with her. And she says she loves me too."

"Do you call *that* bad?"

"It is if I don't want to marry her."

"Don't you?"

"I do and don't."

"Why?"

"That's just it. I don't know that either." He ran both hands through his hair. "I'll never find anyone like her. I can see myself growing old with her. If I don't act soon, I'll lose her forever. But I keep telling myself that I can't."

"Do you feel you're not good enough for her?"

"Of *course* I'm not good enough for her. But that's not it."

"What is it, then?"

"I must be crazy! Do you think I'm crazy?"

"I wouldn't say crazy."

"What *would* you say? That I can't handle responsibility?"

I pulled at my beard and considered him. "I happen to know your advisor, Zack. He has nothing but good to say about your senior thesis. And last year, when you ran the Speakers Program for the Student Christian Council, I heard that you were the best chairman they'd ever had. So it isn't that you can't handle responsibility." Zack said nothing. "I think you're just afraid to grow up."

"I'm *terrified* to grow up," he blurted. "Lots of my friends are too — some of them even more than me. Except they don't know it, or else they think it's normal. Why are so many people like that?"

"A better question would be, 'Why are *you* like that?'"

"I don't know. I guess I think I'll make a mess of things." He changed the subject. "Were people of your age afraid of growing up?"

"Lots of them are still afraid of growing up," I said.

"Has it always been that way?"

"I'd say no. Historically, there have always been some people who have been afraid of growing up, but most have looked forward to it. Prolonged adolescence is an invention of recent times."

"How recent?"

"Fifties or sixties, I'd say."

"Your generation?"

"Yes, we have a lot to answer for."

"What made it different from the generations before it?"

"Lots of things."

"Like what?"

"Too many to list them all."

"List some of them."

I sighed. "Too much free time. Too few responsibilities. Too much disposable income. Enormous high schools in which teens imitated each other instead of grown-ups. Mass higher education for people who weren't really interested in it. Separation of the generations as families moved around to catch economic opportunities. Loss of traditions. Rise of 'experts.' Decline of Christian faith. Resulting loss of the eternal perspective. With that, an increasing inability to set distant goals even for *this* life. That's just for starters."

"What do you mean, 'just for starters'?"

"I mean that there's an even bigger reason for the change."

"What?"

"The collapse of sexual mores. And with that went something else: the ancient, tacit covenant among all women. You see, once enough young women stopped holding out for marriage, the bargaining position of the ones who did hold out was undercut. As my grandmother said, 'Why buy the cow if you can get the milk for free?'"

"Like most of my friends do."

"But the next part of the story concerns you particularly."

"How do you mean?"

"The other big result of sexual laxity was that divorce rates shot up like rockets. This had all sorts of bad effects. A child idealizes his parents. *If* they *can't stay married*, he thinks, *then how could I?* He may even blame himself for the divorce. And so he expects to make a mess of things, as adults always do."

Zack looked stricken.

"Worse yet, lots of divorces mean that lots of kids grow up without dads. If a boy's father deserts his mother, the very idea of fatherhood is diminished in his eyes. That's a catastrophe, and I don't just mean that he's sad. To a small boy, his father is more than his father—he's his vision of the future, his portrait of adult manhood. If that vision is discredited, then growing up itself is discredited."

The stricken look on Zack's face continued to deepen.

"This sense of disillusionment spreads through the—"

"Please stop, Professor T."

"I'm sorry."

"No, it's okay. I just need to stop listening for a minute." We finished our sandwiches. I asked for an espresso. Zack signaled for a refill on his soft drink. He set it down, took a long breath, and exhaled. We looked at each other. "So how does a guy—"

"A *man*, Zack. You're twenty-two."

"I don't feel like one."

"But you are one."

"Then how does a . . . *man* . . . of twenty-two start growing up?"

I thought for a little while. "There are two main things. One was known even to the pagans. The other is a mystery of Christian faith."

"Go on."

"The thing that even the pagans knew is that in order to grow up, you've got to start acting like a grown-up. It's the same with every trait of character. To become courageous, you practice the actions of courageous people. To become frank and openhearted, you practice the actions of frank and openhearted people. Whatever you do consistently, for good or ill, you become."

His brow furrowed. "That sounds circular."

"Think about it."

"What's the other one—the Christian thing?"

"Your earthly model of manhood may have been defective, even absent, but a flawless man once walked on earth and reigns in heaven, from which He will return in power. Focus your gaze on the perfect

Manhood of the perfect Father's Son. Study it, pray about it, meditate on it—and copy it."

For a long time Zack looked at me goggle-eyed. Then he collected himself, folded his arms, and smirked. "So you say. But if I'm supposed to do that, then what's Julie supposed to do?"

I wasn't about to be sidetracked. "For one thing, Zack," I said, "she can hold you to it."

GIRL AND GUY LETTERS

DOES IT MATTER WHO YOU LIVE WITH?

Dear Professor Theophilus:

I cannot possibly see how it is wrong or unbiblical to rent an apartment with a person of the opposite sex. We're close, but I can honestly say that we've never thought about sleeping with each other.

Reply: I don't believe you, but thanks for writing.

Is that all you have to say to me?

I don't think you should believe yourself either.

You're not taking me seriously.

I am taking you seriously, but you aren't taking the difference between males and females seriously. Here are some more considerations:

1. You may tell me that you've never thought about sex, but if you're the girl and he's the guy, you can be sure that he has.

2. You may tell me that you've never thought about sex, but if you're the girl, you can't tell me that you've never thought about romance.

3. If you're the guy, ask yourself this question: You've just learned that before meeting you, your sweetheart lived for three years with Brad Pitt. She says sex never even crossed their minds. Do you believe her?

4. Sex or no sex, thoughts or no thoughts, the situation is inherently unchaste; it corrodes the virtue of modesty. I suppose you'll tell me that you've never eaten breakfast or watched TV together in your pajamas or hung your intimate clothing over the shower rail to dry.

5. It's wrong not only to commit sin, but also to give the appearance of committing sin. Doing so shows lack of love for others because you're demoralizing them through bad example.

6. You wanted Bible, so here's Bible. Modesty is a biblical virtue; it's a
   biblical precept to avoid not only evil, but also the appearance of
   evil; and avoiding not only sin, but also the risk of sin, is a counsel
   of biblical wisdom: "Can a man scoop fire into his lap without his
   clothes being burned? Can a man walk on hot coals without his feet
   being scorched?" (Proverbs 6:27-28).

Grace and peace,
Professor Theophilus

MISSIONARY DATING

Dear Professor Theophilus:

*I've never before read a column of yours that I didn't agree with. I believe that any type
of sexual behavior outside of marriage is wrong in every circumstance and that the sole
purpose of dating is to find a suitable marriage partner. But my mind is boggling over
"Does It Matter Who You Date?" If I understand you correctly, meeting a guy for coffee is, by definition, a romantic date, despite our own feelings to the contrary. Is it sexually immoral to spend time with guys?*

Reply: Wow, you move fast. Let's slow that down and break it up!

Is meeting a guy for coffee, by definition, a date?

"Date. An appointment or engagement at a particular time, frequently with
a person of the opposite sex; a social activity engaged in by two persons
of opposite sex" (Oxford English Dictionary, second edition, 1989).

But COFFEE?

Is there something about the aroma of a coffee house that builds anti-
bodies against the development of romance? I invite letters from readers who have had romantic coffee dates.

Are all dates romantic?

Obviously not—at first. But one thing leads to another, and there is no kind of "liking" between a man and a woman that is unaffected by the fact that they are of opposite sex.

So is it sexually immoral to spend time with guys?

C'mon, you know I didn't say that. Try again.

I mean, is it BAD to spend time with guys?

I didn't say that either. There are lots of ways to spend time with guys besides dating. Try again.

I mean, is it bad to DATE guys?

Dating is fine, but save it for men it would be okay to fall in love with—which, translated, is men it would be all right to marry. Didn't you say in your letter that the sole purpose of dating is to find a suitable marriage partner?

So you're saying I CAN spend time alone with THOSE guys, right?

You're getting closer, but even with the guys it's okay to date, you should sharply limit your time alone. It's at this point that sex comes into the picture. (Remember? You wanted to bring it up before.) The more hours you spend alone together, the more likely you are to end up horizontal, no matter how firmly you had intended abstinence.

You speak as though we don't have any rational control over ourselves.

Not at all. We have rational control, and we should work to strengthen it. But we should be realistic about its weaknesses. Your rational control is:

1. Strong in deciding what circumstances to put yourself in;
2. Weak in deciding what emotions to have when you're already in those circumstances; and
3. Weakest in deciding what to do when you are already under the influence of those emotions.

For this reason, I emphasize decision 1. You want to put all your eggs in the other two baskets. Sheesh.

Grace and peace,
Professor Theophilus

I WANNA BE EQUAL WITH HER

Dear Professor Theophilus:

I am a college guy who has never done anything more than make out with a few girls. Recently I met a girl who I like incredibly, but she had sex with a previous boyfriend. She repented long before she met me and doesn't want to have sex any more till marriage.

I've struggled severely with this issue, crying and praying many nights. I have continual images in my mind of them having sex. I have never met the guy, but he is a big football player, and I am a small computer nerd.

My girlfriend wants to wait till marriage before we even get to the "touchy stage," but I want to have some of our own moments to replace the images in my mind. I would rather face our wedding day as a nonvirgin with my girlfriend because then we would be entering the day as equals. If the husband is supposed to be the spiritual head of the wife, how am I supposed to let her deceive everyone, including our parents, into thinking that she is pure while I do not bear the same mark? I would like to be responsible for her.

Only after I started dating her did I have desires to have sex before marriage. I always thought it should be reserved for the wedding day, but in our case it is different. I told her I wanted to elope, but she will not accept that. I can wait years before I propose to her, but I would like to gradually build up our physical bond with the summation of that bond being total sex when we get married. I have very good brakes and have been making out with her for a long time and am in complete control at all times. These brakes are strong because I have put on the brakes two other times when previous girlfriends wanted to have sex.

What do you recommend?

Thanks,
Someone who just wants to do the biblical thing

Reply: Your letter sets off ten screaming sirens in my mind. Let's go through them systematically.

1. "I've struggled severely with this issue, crying and praying many nights. I have continual images in my mind of them having sex."

Your anguish is understandable, and I cannot offer hope that it will pass away. Until and unless it does, though, don't consider marriage with the girl. If you do enter marriage with these feelings, the prognosis for the marriage will be poor.

2. "I always thought [sex] should be reserved for the wedding day, but in our case it is different." Everyone thinks his case is different. Everyone thinks he has a good reason. Stop telling lies to yourself.

3. "I can wait years before I propose to her, but I would like to gradually build up our physical bond with the summation of that bond being total sex when we get married." Translation: "I want every part of sex but penetration. So long as I get more and more of that, I don't need to get married for a long, long time." You make this sound like a testimony to your self-control. Actually, it's a testimony to your lack thereof.

4. "I have very good brakes; I have been making out with her for a long time and am in complete control at all times." Translation: "I don't have a license to drive, but I refuse to wait. My compromise is to ram on the accelerator with my right foot, while ramming on the brake with my left. Smell that rubber burn! Aren't you impressed that I can keep the car from moving forward?" No, what makes the greatest impression on me is that you haven't the slightest idea what a car is for. Cars are for driving. Until you get that license, don't even start the ignition.

5. "These brakes are strong because I have put on the brakes two other times when previous girlfriends wanted to have sex." Translation: "I view sexual arousal as just another form of recreation. So long as we don't have penetration, I call that putting on the brakes." A better name for it is *not* putting on the brakes. Sexual arousal isn't recreation — it's foreplay. Between spouses about to have intercourse, it's pure. Between you and your girlfriends, it's not.

6. "I told her I wanted to elope, but she will not accept that." Nor should she; elopement would be an insult to her family and yours and a disgrace to the meaning of marriage. Marriage is a mutual and irrevocably binding promise between the spouses to live as husband and wife, entered into in the sight of God and the community of faith who are assembled as witnesses so they can hold you to your vows.

7. "My girlfriend wants to wait till marriage before we even get to the 'touchy stage,' but I want to have some of our own moments to replace the images in my mind." Translation: "She sinned with that other stud, so I won't be satisfied until she sins with me." You say you love her, but love is a commitment of the will to the true good of the other party. I can't find the slightest sign of a commitment of your will to her good.

8. "I would rather face our wedding day as a nonvirgin with my girlfriend because then we would be entering the day as equals." You're certainly right that you aren't yet equals; she is your moral superior. She has repented of her sexual sin, but you can't wait to sin more. The kind of "equality" you want is to drag her back down to your level.

9. "If the husband is supposed to be the spiritual head of the wife, how am I supposed to let her deceive everyone, including our parents, into thinking that she is pure while I do not bear the same mark? I would like to be responsible for her." Give me a break. Nobody "leads" by sinning. Besides, if she has truly repented, then the only "mark" on her is Christ's.

10. "Someone who just wants to do the biblical thing" The biblical thing is just what you *don't* want to do. Try as I might, I can find nothing in your letter but habitual lust and self-deception.

My advice is that you abase yourself before God and beg Him in the name of Christ to make a pure and honest man of you. He can do it; the question is whether you will let Him.

Grace and peace,
Professor Theophilus

WHAT IF WE LOVE EACH OTHER?

Dear Professor Theophilus:

I have a question that may sound a little bit hypocritical coming from a follower of Jesus, but I wanted to ask someone I could trust—someone who didn't know me and wouldn't release my name.

I have attended a Christian school for most of my life, I go to a wonderful church, and my family all love and serve the Lord. My girlfriend was responsible for getting me to join my current church; she is truly my gift from God.

This brings me to my point. My girlfriend and I have been together for nearly a year now and would get married if not for our remaining years in college. She can envision our future together, as can I, as ordained by God and blessed by our pastor. We recently decided to engage in sexual intercourse. We both had questions about our decision to do this, and we both decided to seek advice before deciding to have sex again. We are truly in love, and we connected spiritually before we even decided to have sex. After intercourse, we felt an even closer bond than ever before. Without a doubt, we are mentally, spiritually, and emotionally married; our marriage is only missing a ring, a preacher, and a church ceremony to make it official.

If we make sure that we use protection, is it really that wrong for us to engage in making love? The Lord frowns on promiscuity, but we are not being promiscuous. The Lord values lifelong commitment, and the two of us are as committed as a couple can be. I would like your opinion on this matter as we are both praying and seeking an answer.

Thank you for your time. God bless.

Reply: I'm glad that you and your girlfriend have decided to seek advice before having sexual intercourse again. Because you've been frank with me and because you've asked me to "lay it on the line" for you, that's exactly what I'll do.

The situation in which you find yourself is not uncommon. You see, whether it's right or not, sexual intercourse tends to produce the same powerful feelings of "rightness." That's one of the reasons your feelings are only a blind guide. An even better reason not to trust your feelings is this: In the Bible, God has plainly reserved sex for marriage. He's made this so clear that there is no possibility of honest mistake. When you had sex, then, you weren't being honest with yourselves about His will. That made your thoughts and feelings even more confused because you had to start playing even more tricks on your conscience to cover up the first one.

However, God has been merciful to you and your girlfriend. He wants what's good for you, so He made you just uncomfortable enough about your excuses to write to me. Let me give you a list of your self-deceptions—of the tricks you've been playing on your conscience.

First trick: Not telling yourselves the truth about commitment. Here's how you know you have a commitment: When you're married, you have one, and when you're not married, you don't. Before the marriage ceremony, everything is reversible—your thoughts, your feelings, even your intention to get married. As a matter of fact, people who have sex outside of marriage usually *don't* wind up marrying each other. Nope, not even when the thought of getting married was their reason for having sex.

Second trick: Not telling yourselves the truth about marriage. Face it: You're not married. Feeling married doesn't make you married; having sex doesn't make you married. What makes you married is a solemn public promise in front of God and the assembly of His people to love, honor, and live with each other as husband and wife until death. The reason you have to do it in front of the rest of your worship community is that at the same time the two of you make a vow before God to each other, all those witnesses make a vow before God to hold you to your promise. You haven't made yours; they haven't made theirs.

Third trick: Not telling yourselves the truth about God's rules. In the Bible, God forbids *all* sex outside of marriage. You've softened this to forbidding "promiscuity." Limiting your sexual disobedience to a single person doesn't turn it into obedience. Neither does limiting it to someone whom you think you would like to marry or to someone with whom you have enjoyed God's blessings in the past. Neither does calling it "making love."

Fourth trick: Not telling yourselves the truth about God's authority. When you tell yourselves that using "protection" will make sexual sin okay, you're trying to go over God's head. You're making a guess about the reason for His rule and then thinking that if you can get around the reason, you don't have to obey the rule. But God hasn't told you, "Use protection." What He's told you is, "Don't have sex outside of marriage." Another way to think of it is this: Anything that turns a precious gift like children into something from which you think you need "protection" must be terribly wrong.

Fifth trick: Not telling yourselves the truth about your own motives. When you ask God in prayer whether it's okay to have sex outside of marriage, you're only pretending because you know He has already answered that question in His Scriptures. You see, God doesn't contradict Himself; He doesn't say one thing in the Bible and another thing when you pray. If He has already told you what to do, then asking Him, "What should I do?" isn't a way to find His will but a way to avoid it. He says to you, "Why do you keep asking me questions I've already answered?"

So what do you do now? Before anything else, you and your girlfriend need to repent. That means admitting to yourselves and to God that you've disobeyed Him; it means admitting to yourselves and to God that you've been playing tricks on your conscience; it means being sorry; it means telling Him that you're sorry; and it means reversing course. If your girlfriend doesn't want to repent, that doesn't get you off the hook; you will just have to repent by yourself. You'll have to do that even if she becomes angry, even if she threatens to break off the relationship, and even if she *does* break off the relationship.

After repenting, ask God to forgive you through Jesus Christ. Then ask Him for strength to resist future sexual temptations because by giving in once, you've made it harder to resist the next time. Finally, agree *now* to avoid tempting situations—situations like being alone together. I'll bet you didn't know that the more time a couple spends alone together, the more likely they are to wind up in bed! That's true even if they begin with a firm intention of abstinence.

By the way, when you and your girlfriend pray to God, you should pray separately; prayer time is probably the worst of all times to be alone together. As Ben Young and Sam Adams write in their book, *The Ten Commandments of Dating,* two of the most powerful drives in human nature are the sex drive and the spiritual drive. If you put both drives together, they'll be too strong for you. There will be plenty of time to pray alone together after you're married.

One last thing: Don't make the deadly mistake of telling yourselves, "We'll sin again, but it will be all right because God will forgive us." Yes, God does forgive, but there is no forgiveness without repentance. By deliberately sinning, you're really training yourselves *not* to repent. If you harden your heart before you sin, how do you know you'll be able to soften it afterward?

Grace and peace,
Professor Theophilus

I GOT MY GIRLFRIEND PREGNANT. WHAT NOW?

Dear Professor Theophilus:

I was wondering if you could offer some advice on a situation I am in at the moment. I am a Christian. I have a nonChristian girlfriend and just recently found out that she is pregnant. I hadn't been sleeping with her beforehand; she got pregnant pretty much the first time we were together (I've been lectured about the use of protection, but we didn't plan for it and were unprepared).

This raises so many issues for us, like whether we should get married, where we should live, where we should live over the summer break (she needs me to be there for her while she's pregnant, and it's my baby too), and how we are going to support ourselves once the baby is born. I've looked into a few things such as government benefits and what we should do about study loads, and I think we a have a rough idea on how things will work out. Our families are very supportive although fairly concerned for us at the same time.

My main question at the moment is about marriage. I believe we should get married, not only because of the baby but because I love her a lot and I know she loves me too. The issue of her not being a Christian is fairly important to me, though, and I don't know how I'm going to tell my friends that I'm married and only nineteen (although I turn twenty next month) because I slept with my girlfriend.

It seems as though there is no single correct answer, but I'd appreciate it if you could help me find the "most correct" answer. I hope you can help me out with some advice or at least point me in the right direction to find the answers. I appreciate your help.

P. S. I'm sort of amazed at myself in some ways. I've read countless articles and books on sex before marriage and firmly believe the benefits in not doing it, but I chose to do it anyway. I guess even if we are fully aware of the consequences, some people still tend to make silly choices. I'm thankful for God's grace at the moment and try to make myself as humble as I can, although at the moment I feel kind of proud of myself. It's something like the feeling you get when you've been doing things without God's help for too long, and I don't particularly enjoy the feeling.

Reply: I will answer your questions—but before you read further, let me ask you to do four things because if you don't, the answers to your questions may not make much difference. Here's why the four things are necessary. You say you know you've "made a silly choice," but you don't acknowledge that you've sinned. "Doing things without God's help" comes closer to an accurate description, but it's not there yet. Sin is grave business. More than being imprudent, it's defying God.

First, you need to call what you did by its right name. It wasn't an error but a sin, and it wasn't "being together" but having sex. While you're at it, notice that you committed two other sins as well. You shouldn't have given the young woman such a rotten example of what it means to follow Christ, and you should have been seeking a spouse who also knew Christ rather than getting mixed up with someone who didn't. What did you think dating was for?

Second, you need to repent of those three sins before God in the name of Jesus Christ. Repentance means more than being sorry—it means turning 180 degrees around and going the other way. Among other things, going the other way means that you renounce having further sex with the young woman outside of marriage; the fact that she's already pregnant doesn't give you a green light to continue. But listen to this: Going the other way does *not* mean that you should abandon her just because you shouldn't have dated or had sex with her in the first place. You have new obligations now. More about that below.

Third, when you repent, you must accept God's forgiveness. He promises it to those who genuinely repent and trust Christ as their sin bearer. This is a guarantee. It isn't godly to berate yourself for your sins and yet not accept His forgiveness; the idea is to repent, accept His forgiveness, and live from henceforth on the path of sanctity.

Fourth, you need to ask His help to do His will for the rest of your life, beginning with what lies immediately ahead.

Have you done these four things? If not, go back and do them.

Now prepare yourself. You ask my help for the situation you are in "at the moment." That is the wrong way to think of it. It isn't for the moment but for the rest of your time on earth. I won't say, "Your life is about to change" because it already has. You are now a father, and you already have the obligations of a father. The fact that the child is not yet born makes no difference. The fact that you didn't intend to become a father makes no difference either. You are one, and from now on your first earthly obligation is to protect the mother and the child.

Should you marry her? You say that you want to, not only because of the baby but because you love each other, but that you're concerned about your youth, what your friends will say, and the fact that she's not a Christian.

Let me address each of these issues in turn.

Marriage: Yes, you should marry her, and you should understand that marriage is permanent. "For better or for worse" means exactly what it says. If you marry thinking, "so long as it works out," it won't. The reason you should marry her is that you are now a father, and God has already made a provision for fathers to protect their families. The marital bond is precisely that provision. If there would be grave impediments to a marriage — for example, if you had another wife, if she had another husband, or if either or both of you were morally incapable of undertaking your marital obligations — then you and the mother should give the child up to be adopted by a Christian husband and wife who can provide a good home. This would be a real sacrifice on your part; it is not easy to do. The alternative, however — relegating the young woman to single momhood with you merely making visits and paying child support — is unthinkable.

Love: Yes, you should love each other, but remember what love is: not a feeling, not an emotion, not a state of romantic excitement, but a commitment of the will to the true good of the other person. Such commitments are sealed by promises; that's what the marriage ceremony is about. The feelings are just gravy, and they may come and go.

Youth: Nineteen is not too young to get married. My wife and I married at nineteen. Nor is twenty too young to have children. We had our first at twenty-one. In our grandparents' day, young men and women married and had children much earlier than today. Our era has merely prolonged adolescence. People take longer to grow up, not because it has to take that long, but because not much is expected of them.

What your friends will say: When you get married, don't say to your friends, "I had to get married because I slept with my girlfriend." Say, "Guess what? I'm married!" What will they say? I hope they will say, "Congratulations!" If they say something else, you need another set of friends—which may very well be the case. You and your wife will probably find yourselves making your closest friends among other young married couples.

The fact that the young woman is not a Christian: It's true—barring other obligations—that Christians should marry other Christians. But that point is moot because you do have other obligations now. You are the father of a child with this woman, and therefore your relationship with her has already changed permanently. You aren't like an uncommitted person considering whether to date a nonbeliever; you are more like a married person considering whether to divorce a nonbeliever—and I hope I don't have to tell you what God thinks of divorce. You are now the young woman's protector and the protector of the child, and as I said, God's provision for this protection is marriage. Now comes the hard part. To be a good protector—a good physical protector and a good spiritual protector—you have to change. You weren't physically protecting the young woman when you had sex with her. (By the way, get rid of the idea that condoms are "protection." They aren't. The only protector is a living being.) And you weren't spiritually protecting her when you gave her such an awful example of what it means to follow Christ. To be the protector of the mother and child, you must now become the man you haven't been so far. My recommendation to you is to get down on your knees every day and beg God to make you that man. So she isn't a follower of Christ? From now on, you are His earthly representative to her. If she does come to know Him, it will probably be because she sees Him in you. If she doesn't, it will probably be because she doesn't see Him in you.

One last point: Life has already changed, but it will change more than you think. You've spoken of government assistance. Are you in poverty? That's not likely; not many poor people are in college. If you aren't, it is shameful to seek government assistance. Are you able-bodied? I thought so. Then work. You may have to go to school part-time or take a break from school. It isn't the end of the world; I did it. You will look back on it and say, "I'm glad I did that." Accepting help from parents is better than accepting help from the government, but remember that you are an adult now, the father of your own new family. So try not to burden your own parents either. My advice is to accept aid for tuition from your parents if they offer it, but so far as possible, provide the living expenses for your new family by your own labors. Your parents may want to help you more than that. Love them for it, but don't agree; it wouldn't be good for you.

I have been tough with you, not from self-righteousness—God knows that I am a great sinner—but because you have a tough road ahead of you. Let me close with two thoughts.

First, you will not make the road any easier by imagining that you can choose another. Be a man of God now, a follower of Christ. Take up His shield and sword as His soldier and face what must be faced with a song of strength and faith.

Second, if you do follow Him, He will bless you. The Lord chastises those He loves, but He will not always chastise. If you accept His chastisement, He will use it to give you goodness that you have never imagined. Read these words of King David, who knew something about repentance and forgiveness.

> *The* LORD *is compassionate and gracious,*
>   *slow to anger, abounding in love.*
> *He will not always accuse,*
>   *nor will he harbor his anger forever;*
> *he does not treat us as our sins deserve*
>   *or repay us according to our iniquities.*
> *For as high as the heavens are above the earth,*
>   *so great is his love for those who fear him;*
> *as far as the east is from the west,*
>   *so far has he removed our transgressions from us.*
>   *(Psalm 103:8-12)*

Grace and peace,
Professor Theophilus

I'M THE GIRLFRIEND

I took some hits for my answer to "I Got My Girlfriend Pregnant." One writer even published an article dishonestly accusing me of claiming that all families are happy, of urging a "shotgun wedding," and of implying that a pregnant woman should marry even the sort of man who would sock her in the stomach. Of course all I really said was that an intact home with two loving parents is preferable to a broken one, that the young man should step up to his responsibility on his own, and that he should be the best dad and husband he can be. Nearly two years later, a young woman wrote to me with a biblical question. She then wrote a second letter that brought tears to my eyes:

When I mentioned to my husband that I'd written you a letter, he said that he, too, had once written with a major question and was surprised that you spent so much time replying. As it turns out, I am the girlfriend of "I Got My Girlfriend Pregnant." I thought you might like to know how everything turned out for us.

Obviously, I don't want to make light of the sin or say that it was ever okay for us to have sex before we were married. However, I believe we have become an example of how God can take a pair of sinners and turn the situation into something that can give others who've made the same mistake some kind of hope. We did get married, even though I was a nonChristian at the time. My own family encouraged me to "just" have an abortion and didn't see why we should marry. In my dad's words, marriage "is just a piece of paper, and I know plenty of happy unmarried couples." (I think his definition of a happy couple is a bit different from mine!) I'm really happy to say that we kept the baby and now have a beautiful fifteen-month-old son. Shortly after his birth, I asked Jesus into my life, and He has totally transformed me and given me peace and purpose that my former life could not offer.

I just want to say that it is only now that I understand why sex outside marriage is so wrong. I really believe that we missed out on something special and important by not waiting until marriage. I hope other young people can listen to someone like me who did things the wrong way and know that it isn't worth the emotional and spiritual stress to give in to some fleeting desire to sleep together outside of marriage. It makes things so much more complicated. It's taken most of the last two years to work through the issues created from premarital sex, and at times this has been a serious burden. I am so thankful for God's grace and willingness to help us even though we disobeyed Him!

I don't want to say that Christians should date nonChristians. I imagine it was quite difficult for my husband, and I'm so glad he was patient enough to give me the time I needed to make the decision but loving enough to keep encouraging me toward Jesus. I don't know how he had the patience to handle my warped beliefs and opinions, and I am ever grateful that God used this situation to see me saved and to ensure that our son would be raised in a loving Christian home.

Anyway, my husband is going to finish his degree in a few weeks, which means he'll soon be able to work full-time. I had to drop to a quarter load of study so that I could stay at home to look after our son without totally dropping out of school.

Well, I guess that's all you need to know. I just thought it might be nice for you to find out what happened because I am under the impression that it is rare for a marriage to last long when it's begun in these circumstances. However, with the help of Christian premarriage counseling and our involvement in a young married couples' Bible study group and a fantastic church, we have found that God has taken our sin and helped us make the most of what we have. I'm just so glad that I now have a loving husband who (despite his mistakes) introduced me to Jesus and a wonderful son whom we are raising as a Christian. I just hope and pray that he will make better decisions than we did!

I suppose all this explains why when I read "I Got My Girlfriend Pregnant" in your archives, I could identify with the author of the letter—I just didn't realize that he was my husband!

FAITH ON CAMPUS STUFF

IF THE REFORMATION'S OVER, CAN WE DANCE?

RELIGIOUS DIPLOMACY BETWEEN THE SEXES.

I was about to eat lunch when someone plopped down at my table at the Edge of Night. "Hi, Professor Theophilus. I wonder — hey, is that *sauerkraut* I see sticking out of your sandwich?"

"Hello, Don. Haven't you ever seen a Reuben sandwich?"

"Seen one? I haven't even heard of one. What is it?" He gave my plate a hungry look and ordered two large pizzas with double cheese and pepperoni.

"A Reuben sandwich, you gastronomical ignoramus, is corned beef and mild German sauerkraut on Jewish rye with Russian dressing."

"German sauerkraut on — yeah. That reminds me of what I wanted to talk to you about."

"I'd say you're dating a girl, and she's either German, Russian, or Jewish."

"Close. She's Catholic, and I'm only thinking about it."

"That's not close."

"Close enough. But I'm Protestant. We met in a pro-life group. What do you think? Could a relationship between us . . . you know, work?"

I laughed. "Why don't you bring me a hard question some time, Don?"

"Sorry."

"I haven't even met her."

"She took your class last semester on — well, maybe I shouldn't let on who she is. But look here, I'm not asking whether she and I could *get along.*"

"Good!"

"I'm just asking the theological question."

"What's 'the theological question'?"

He stalled. "Well, I know that believers should marry only other believers. Second Corinthians six-something."

"Six-fourteen."

"And I know that applies to dating, too, because dating is about finding a suitable marriage partner."

"Glad to hear you agree. So what's your question?"

He looked embarrassed. "Are Catholics Christians?"

I winced. "Has someone been telling you that they *can't* be?"

"Yeah, my grandfather Smaczny. I figured he ought to know because he used to be Catholic himself."

"What made him decide Catholics aren't Christians?"

"Old family story. When he was little in Poland, he was taught that you earn your way into heaven by being good. He was always afraid that he wouldn't make the grade and would wind up in hell. When he moved here he lived with his aunt. She showed him in the Bible where Paul says we're 'justified by faith in Christ and not by observing the law.' When he asked the priest about it, the priest got angry and threw him out. So his eyes were opened, and he converted."

I didn't speak. Don waved his hand in front of my eyes. "Prof? You awake?"

"I was considering how to answer you."

"Don't worry, Professor T. I'm pretty hard to insult."

I laughed wryly. "That's the least of my worries."

"Well, then?"

"All right, let's start from the beginning. Because of our rebellion, we humans are in a desperate situation. Not only are we separated from

God, but nothing we can do by our own power can bridge the infinite gap. *He* provides the bridge in Jesus Christ."

"Yeah, I know all that."

"When Christ died on the cross, what He was doing was putting Himself in our place—taking upon Himself the penalty that we deserved but couldn't pay. You understand that too?"

"Sure. Basic Christian stuff."

"Right. So what it means to be a Christian is to let the Rescuer rescue you, to put your whole faith and trust in Him as the one who bears your sins for you. He's the rope. Faith is joining all the people who are holding onto it. Now do you see what that implies?"

"That rescue is a gift?"

"Right. You become acceptable to God not because He accepts something you do for Him, but because you accept something He does for you. Trustfully accepting it—that's what faith is. As theologians put it, we're justified by grace through faith—we're made right with God by a pure gift that is accepted through pure trust."

"But what about Catholics?" Don asked.

"I'm getting to that. A Catholic who trustingly accepts God's grace through Christ is justified in exactly the same way as a Protestant who trustingly accepts God's grace through Christ. Now your grandfather's charge was that a good Catholic *can't* do that. He thought the Catholic Church *denies* what we've just been saying—*denies* that justification is a gift and claims we *can* earn our way into heaven. Of course that's the same thing Martin Luther thought in the days when Protestants first broke away from Rome."

"Yeah, I hear about that every year on Reformation Sunday. Grampa loves that day. He feels the same way about Reformation Sunday that kids do about Christmas. So wasn't Luther right?"

"It's true that in 1563 at the Council of Trent, the Catholic Church did seem to confirm Luther's charge by declaring, 'If anyone says that the sinner is justified by faith alone . . . let him be anathema,' which means 'condemned.'"

"I know that too."

"But it's not so simple."

"What do you mean? What could be simpler than the Reformers saying, 'Justification is by faith alone' and the Catholics saying, 'No, it's not'?"

I sighed. "In the first place, Protestants and Catholics have sometimes used the word *justification* in different senses. So when the Reformers said, 'Yes' and Trent said, 'No,' it's not clear that Trent was denying precisely the same thing that the Reformers were affirming."

He thought for a moment. "Then what about my grandfather? You don't think he was lying about what he was taught, do you?"

"No, I don't. But you know, Don, your family isn't the only one that hands down old stories. A couple of weeks ago a Catholic student told me a story *her* family had handed down. *Her* grandfather had grown up *Protestant*. One day when he was a young man — it was a weekday — he walked into the church without notice and found the deacon in the arms of a young woman who wasn't his wife. When he confronted the man, the deacon replied, 'You can't judge me. I'm justified by faith alone.' She ended her story just as you ended yours: 'So his eyes were opened, and he converted.'"

Don was horrified. "But justification by grace through faith doesn't mean you can do anything you want!"

"That's my point. Huge gaps can open up between what a doctrine really means and what filters down to the people in the pews. That happens in both Protestant and Catholic churches. In the name of Catholic doctrine, your grandfather was taught that we earn our way into heaven; in the name of Protestant doctrine, her grandfather was taught that because we *don't*, it doesn't matter how we live. The former isn't authentic Catholic doctrine any more than the latter is authentic

ASK ME ANYTHING   75

Protestant doctrine."

"It *isn't* Catholic doctrine?"

"No."

"How do you know that?"

"In recent times, the Catholic Church has officially declared that justification *is* by grace through faith."

"Really?"

"Sure. Have you ever heard of the Joint Declaration on the Doctrine of Justification?"

"No. Is that something new?"

"It was signed only recently, but it's been in the works for years."

"Who signed it?"

"Representatives of the World Lutheran Federation and the Roman Catholic Church. Guess when."

"I haven't a clue."

"October 31, 1999 — Reformation Day."

"No kidding! What does it say?"

I laughed. "It's pretty long, Don. You can read it later on the Internet. But the key point is this: Both sides agreed that 'by grace alone, in faith in Christ's saving work and not because of any merit on our part, we are accepted by God and receive the Holy Spirit, who renews our hearts while equipping and calling us to good works.'¹ Although they still disagreed about the details, they agreed about the essentials and declared that the mutual condemnations of the Reformation era no longer apply to the partners in the discussion."

Don gaped. "Then is the Reformation over?"

For a few moments I couldn't answer; I was trying to hold in both laughter and tears. "I'm sorry, Don," I said finally. "*That's* going to take somewhat longer."

"Why?"

"In the first place, the World Lutheran Federation can't even speak for all Lutherans, much less all Protestants. Much more work is necessary before everyone can be brought to agree. In the second place, the Joint Declaration concerns only the biggest of the issues that divide Catholics and Protestants—there are still lots of others."

"Then what *does* the Declaration accomplish? Anything?"

"Yes! Yes! It accomplishes an answer to the question you asked me at the beginning."

Don looked sheepish. "What question was that? I forgot."

"You asked whether Catholics can be Christians."

"And the answer is—?"

"It's 'Yes!' Of course there may be a good many Catholics who misunderstand Catholic doctrine and put their trust in their own efforts instead of in the sacrifice of Christ—just as there may be a good many Protestants who misunderstand Protestant doctrine and think you can do anything you want. But if we consider what the two sides *officially teach*, the problem is gone."

"I understand that."

"And it's gone on *both sides*, which is very important."

"On both sides? Now you're losing me again."

"Think of it this way. Protestants need assurance that the Catholic Church understands that we can't earn our way into heaven and that our reconciliation with God is a pure gift accepted by pure trust. I think the Declaration gives them that. But don't forget that *Catholics* also need a certain assurance about *Protestants*."

"They do?"

"Sure. They need assurance that Protestants understand that a faith unaccompanied by a reformation of life isn't genuine faith at all and that there can't be any advance in holiness without Christian discipline. I think the Declaration gives them that too."

Don's eyes lit up. "If Catholics can be Christians, then the Catholic girl I told you about—well, I'd have to find out if she really gets it about not earning our way into heaven—"

"Yes, and she'd have to find out whether *you* really get it about living a holy life—"

"Oh, sure—but if we did that and we happened to get serious about each other, then we *could* make a marriage work."

"I didn't say that you could make a marriage work!"

"You mean we couldn't?"

"I didn't say that either! Who am I to prophesy? It's just that it's not easy to make a marriage work even between a Presbyterian and a Pentecostal, and they're both Protestants! Besides, it isn't fair to the children for the parents to disagree over religious questions; they're likely to grow up agnostics."

"So where does that leave us?"

"I think you and the girl simply have a lot of things to talk about. You're going to have to find out what you can and can't agree on."

Don pondered. "Well, Prof," he said finally, "don't be surprised if I show up again asking you to explain purgatory or saints or sacraments or something."

"Okay," I replied, grinning. Don popped the last two pieces of pizza into his mouth, swallowed, waved, and shot out the door.

Just as I was returning to my long-forgotten Reuben sandwich, I sensed someone at my shoulder. Looking up, I recognized a tall young woman I had taught before. "Professor Theophilus?"

"At your service—oh, good to see you!"

"Do you remember me? I was in your Comparative Religion class last semester."

"Of course. We talked about some Christian things during office hours one day. What's up?"

Although she was a lot better looking, she plopped down exactly the way Don does. A hunch stole into my mind. "Well, it's like this. I'm Catholic, but I met this nice Protestant boy in my pro-life group, and I think he's interested in me. So what I'm wondering is"—my hunch grew stronger—"are Protestants Christians?"

A SKEPTICAL VIEW OF CHRISTIANITY

I DIDN'T SAY SKEPTICAL *ABOUT* CHRISTIANITY.

"Professor?"

"Hmm?" I said. "Oh, hello, Mark. What can I do for you?"

"Are you busy?"

"Looks like I'm about to be."

He began to back out of the office. "Sorry, I guess I should have called first—"

"No, no—I meant busy with you. Did you want to talk about something?"

"Yes. Christianity. You're the only Christian professor I know."

"What's your question?"

"I've been wondering if I'm stupid or something."

I lifted an eyebrow. "You did fine in my course last semester."

"That was different. I'm wondering if I'm stupid to have faith."

"Faith about what? Whether the Resurrection really happened— something like that?"

"No. My problem isn't with faith in this or that—it's with faith in general. I feel like I'm being bombarded."

"Why?"

"The other day my journalism prof quoted a writer who said Christians are 'uneducated and easily led.' This morning my physics TA said he's an atheist because science demands proof and there's no proof of God. My dormitory RA said the difference between philosophy and religion is that religion depends on faith and philosophy depends on reasoning. All these people seem to be saying the same thing."

"And that thing is—?"

"That faith isn't intellectually honest. That the only stance worthy of an intelligent person is skepticism."

"Let's start there. What's skepticism?"

Mark shifted in his seat. "Doubting everything, I suppose."

I smiled. "There's your first mistake."

"Already?"

"You say a skeptic doubts everything. What would it be like to doubt everything?"

"It would make you cautious. Instead of accepting things blindly, you'd reason. You wouldn't be taken in by falsehoods."

"Are you sure? If you doubted everything, wouldn't you doubt the good of caution too?"

"Hmm. I guess you would."

"And if you doubted everything, wouldn't you doubt whether reasoning works?"

"I suppose that's true too. But like I said, doubting everything would keep you from being taken in by falsehoods. Wouldn't it?"

"Yes, but wouldn't it also keep you from being 'taken in' by truths?"

"Why do you say that?"

"You can't know a truth unless you believe it, and you can't believe it if you're doubting it."

He considered that. "I see. If I doubt everything, I can't even know that two plus two equals four."

"Exactly."

"So in order to know anything, eventually I have to stop doubting."

"Right. As the great G. K. Chesterton said, 'Merely having an open mind is nothing. The object of opening the mind, as of opening the mouth, is to shut it again on something solid.'"[1]

"Then is doubt *bad*?"

"No, you just have to know when to stop. The purpose of opening the mind is—"

"To shut it again on something solid."

"But you can't shut it on something solid unless—"

"You open it first."

"Do you understand?"

"I think so." He paused. "Doubt might push me to find a truth, but once I find it I should believe it."

"Exactly. A way of life based on permanent doubt would be senseless."

"Okay, I see that. Maybe skepticism is just demanding that things be put to the test."

"Okay. So?"

"So faith is out. If the choice is between testing things and taking them on faith, I think I should test them."

"I think so too."

"You do?"

I adjusted my glasses. "Of course."

"But that's not Christian."

"Why not? The apostle Paul said, 'Test everything.'"

"Really?"

"Check it out. First Thessalonians chapter five, verse twenty-one."

"Now you're making it sound like Christians are skeptics!"

"We are, Mark—in a way."

"Then I'm confused."

"Start at the beginning. You just said skepticism means demanding that things be put to the test, right?"

"Right."

"Now in order to test anything you have to have a standard, don't you?"

"How so?"

"How do you test whether a mineral is hard or soft?"

"You compare it with another mineral whose hardness you already know."

"How do you test whether someone is a real expert or an imposter?"

"You have him questioned by people whose expertise you trust."

"How do you test whether a claim about the past is true?"

"You see whether the evidence supports it."

"How do you test whether an argument is logically valid?"

"You check it against rules of good reasoning, like, 'Don't contradict yourself.'"

"Do you see where I'm going?" He shook his head. "In every case, you test the thing you're less sure about by using something you're more sure about. That's your standard."

"And you say Christians have testing standards too?"

"Sure. For example, the Bible includes at least nine tests just for the authenticity of alleged gifts of the Holy Spirit."[2]

"I didn't know that."

"Not many people do."

"Okay, suppose I'm testing a mineral or an expert or something. How do I know whether I can trust my standard?"

"What do you think?"

"Test the standard?"

"Right."

"How?"

"With a higher standard."

"Could you give me an example, Prof?"

"Sure. Students are tested by teachers, but teachers are tested by certifiers. Or try this one: The claim about the past is tested by the evidence, but the evidence is tested by the rules of the historical profession."

"But then where does faith come in?"

I laughed. "Consider: You test A by using B, you test B by using C, you test C by using D—don't you see a problem here?"

"Well, sure. The chain has to end somewhere—at some Highest Standard. Or else you haven't really tested anything at all."

"Right. There has to be something absolutely trustworthy, something you trust not for the sake of some still higher standard, but—"

"I guess for itself."

"*That's* where faith comes in."

"Why?"

"You have to accept the Highest Standard on faith because there isn't any higher one to test it with and the chain can't go on forever."

"So demanding that things be tested *doesn't* rule out faith."

"Nope. In fact, it depends on faith."

"I sure didn't expect that."

"It is a little mind-boggling."

"But faith in what?"

"We ought to give absolute trust only to what deserves trust absolutely."

"What deserves trust absolutely?"

"God does. So does His revelation—in His Word and in the structures of His creation."

"But secular people don't believe in God."

"No, they don't. At least they don't *trust* Him."

"So does that mean they can't test things?"

"Not at all. Like everyone, they use what they trust more to test what they trust less."

"But—for them, there's nothing at the end of their chain. They don't have a Highest Standard."

"Sure they do. They just end the chain too soon."

"What do you mean?"

"A secular person treats as the Highest Standard something that isn't the Highest Standard. He puts faith in something that can't support his faith."

"What kind of thing do you mean?"

"Usually something God has made. He trusts the *creature* instead of the Creator."

Mark looked blank. "Could you give an example?"

"Sure. Let's take the TA in your physics class. What do you think he'd say about miracles?"

"He'd reject them, of course."

"And why?"

"He'd say they violate the laws of nature."

"So his standard for testing belief in miracles is—"

"The laws of nature."

"How does he test his standard?"

"I don't think he does test it. He said once in class that 'nature is all there is.' When I asked him how he knew, he said, 'It just is.'"

"So are the laws of nature his Highest Standard?"

"I guess they are."

"Then that's where he places his faith."

"I think he'd be surprised to hear himself described as a man of faith."

I smiled again. "I'm sure he would."

"But don't Christians believe in the laws of nature too?"

"Certainly, but they aren't our highest standard. The Creator is. If He made the laws of nature, He can suspend them."

Mark glanced at his watch. "This conversation has helped me a lot. I have to go. But I'm still not sure how to deal with the bombardment."

"There's no formula, but maybe I can offer a few suggestions. Tell me again what your bombardiers said."

"My journalism professor quoted a writer who said Christians are 'uneducated and easily led.'"

"You can tell him, 'If that were true, I'd believe you right away.'"

"Isn't that just being humorous?"

"Sometimes you can use humor to make a point."

"Then my physics TA said he's an atheist because science demands proof and there's no proof of God."

"Ask him what proof he has that there isn't any."

"Doesn't that reduce everything to the level of 'I say, you say'?"

"Sure it does, if you stop there. I'm not suggesting a way to end the conversation but a way to begin it. He needs to realize that he has a faith commitment too."

"What about what my dorm RA said?"

"What did he say again?"

"That the difference between philosophy and religion is that religion depends on faith but philosophy depends on reasoning."

"Pshaw. Reasoning itself depends on faith."

"How could *that* be?"

"Think. What do you do to construct a defense of reasoning?"

"You reason. What else can you do?"

"So you defend reasoning by reasoning?"

"Right."

"Then your defense is circular. It proves that reasoning works only if you already know that reasoning works."

"So reasoning can't justify itself!"

"Right. You have to accept reasoning by faith. The only question is the one you asked earlier: 'Faith in what?'"

Mark glanced at his watch again, began to stand up, and then sat back down. For a few moments he didn't speak. Then he asked, "If I have more questions, can I come back?"

I grinned. "Anytime you like."

WHY SHOULD I BELIEVE MY BELIEF?

WHAT YOU DIDN'T KNOW YOU KNEW.

Peter had stopped by to ask what I'd be teaching next semester. None of my planned courses fit his schedule (which didn't seem to surprise him), so he seemed to be ready to leave.

But he didn't. Each time he stood up, he thought of some trivial question, then sat down again to ask it. He'd get leg cramps if he kept this up. "Why don't you tell me what's really on your mind?" I asked.

"What do you mean? I wanted to know what you were teaching next semester, and—"

"But you knew that already. And you didn't really come here to ask about the Semester in Uzbekistan or the Internship in Antinomianism."

"What are you, psychic or something?"

I grinned. "Yes."

"Well," he said, "there *is* something I've been wondering about. It's not why I'm here. But since you bring it up, I guess I might as well tell you."

"You might as well," I agreed.

"I was talking with my friend Don. You know him."

"Sure. It's through him that I know you."

"Well, the other day he asked whether I believe in God, and I didn't know what to tell him."

"You don't know whether God is real?"

"It's not that. I don't know whether I believe in Him."

"Isn't that the same thing?"

"No. See, I do believe in God. But I don't see why my belief should be true. So maybe I don't believe in Him, if you see what I mean."

"Maybe you're trying to say that your belief doesn't reflect real *knowledge*, so even though you believe in God, you also think maybe you shouldn't. Am I getting warm?"

"Yeah, that's it. See, one of my other professors said that the only reason I believe in God is that I've been brought up that way. If I'd been brought up by pagans, I'd probably believe in lots of gods. If I'd been brought up by atheists, I probably wouldn't believe in any. So I *have* this belief—but so what?"

I reached for my coffee. "Peter, tell me something."

"What?"

"What makes you sure that you believe in God only because you've been brought up that way?"

He gave me a funny look. "Because I *was* brought up that way. My dad and mom said God made the world, and I believed them."

"Did they also teach you that one plus one equals two and two plus two equals four?"

"Sure."

"Would you say that you believe *those* things just because you were brought up that way?"

He hesitated. "No-o. Because I could see for myself that what they said was true. When I put a penny with a penny, I got two pennies."

"So the mere fact that you were brought up to believe something—"

"—doesn't show that I don't have other reasons to believe it. Right. But that's just it. 'One plus one equals two' is different from 'God made the world.' I have other reasons to believe in one plus one, but I don't have other reasons to believe in God. My parents said God made the world, I believed them, and it stuck. It seems to me that's all."

"Did you believe everything they told you?"

"Well, no."

"For instance?"

"They told me that if I lost a tooth and put it under my pillow, the tooth fairy would come while I was sleeping and leave a quarter in its place."

"Why didn't you believe them about that?"

"I could never see what use a fairy would have for a tooth. Besides, some of my friends got dollars for their teeth and others didn't get anything. Then one day I lost a tooth and forgot to tell my parents, and that night the tooth fairy didn't come. So I decided the tooth fairy must be Mom and Dad."

"Very astute. So you believed your parents when what they told you made sense of other things you knew, but not when it didn't?"

"I guess so. 'One plus one equals two' fit in fine with what I knew about adding pennies. But the tooth fairy didn't fit in with how some kids got dollars and others got nothing, and it didn't fit in with the time I forgot to tell my parents I'd lost a tooth."

"It didn't fit in with what you knew about motives either."

"What do you mean?"

"You knew that nobody does anything without a reason. Otherwise it wouldn't have worried you that you couldn't see what use a fairy would have for a tooth."

"I guess I did know that about motives. It's funny to think of a little kid knowing something like 'Nobody does anything without a reason.'" He grinned. "I must have been pretty smart, huh?"

"Children know more about some things than we give them credit for. So when your parents told you God made the world, what other facts did *this* claim fit in with?"

"I can't think of any at all."

"Tell me this, then. Did they tell you out of the blue that God made the world, or was it the answer to some question?"

"It was the answer to a question. I asked, 'Who made the world?'"

"So it *did* fit in with something you already knew."

"What?"

"You already knew that someone had made the world."

"I *didn't* know that. I just *thought* it."

"All right. But why did you think it?"

"Because even a kid knows that the world must have come from *somewhere*."

"Why?"

"Because there's got to be some good reason for everything."

"That's a rough paraphrase of what philosophers call the principle of sufficient reason—that anything that doesn't *have to be* requires a cause sufficient to account for the effect. So you're saying that even as a child, you had intuitive knowledge of the principle of sufficient reason."

"I guess that is what I'm saying, Prof."

"And you had intuitive knowledge that the world is not the sort of thing that 'has to be.'"

"That too. Hey, my kid self is looking smarter and smarter."

"So it is. But there must have been at least one more thing you knew in those days."

"Why do you say that?"

"Because you didn't ask *what* made the world—you asked *who* made it."

"I don't think that means anything. That's just how kids think. They don't know about impersonal stuff like electromagnetism. They only know about personal stuff like Mom baking cookies."

"A lot of people make that claim. But are you sure it's true? Think back to your own childhood. Suppose your father had been reading an art book to you and had asked, 'Where did this picture come from?' How would you have answered?"

"I would have said, 'Someone colored it.'"

"And would you have thought 'someone' was a person?"

"Yes."

"But now suppose you had been taking a walk with your father after a rainstorm and he had asked, 'Where did this big puddle come from?' How would you have answered this time?"

"I would have said, 'The rain.'"

"And would you have thought the rain was a person?"

"No."

"So you knew the difference between personal and impersonal causes after all."

"Now that you put it that way, I guess I did."

"So what made you think that a personal rather than an impersonal cause made the world—that it was made by a *who* and not a *what?*"

Peter reflected. "I guess the world must have seemed more like a picture than a puddle."

"That's a pretty deep intuition. So you're telling me that even as a child, you understood that some things might be due to impersonal causes, but other things could be brought about only by persons?"

"I guess I am saying that. That's pretty amazing. I sure didn't *know* I knew that stuff."

"We call that kind of knowledge 'latent' or 'implicit.' Latent knowledge is all that you know without being aware that you know it."

"There must be a lot of latent knowledge, then."

"There is. In fact, to ask *who* made the world and not *what* made the world, you would have needed at least one more piece of latent knowledge. It wouldn't have been enough to know *that* some things require personal causes and others don't."

"Um . . . right. I would have had to know *how to tell* which things need personal causes and which ones don't. Because I already knew that the world was one of them."

"Correct."

"But Professor T—"

"Yes?"

"If you asked me *how* I know which things need personal causes, I couldn't tell you."

"All that means is that your knowledge is still partly latent. It doesn't mean that it isn't knowledge."

"But wouldn't I make mistakes now and then? Wouldn't I sometimes get things that do need personal causes mixed up with things that don't?"

"No doubt you would. Anyone might. For example, an archeologist digs up all sorts of things, and usually he can tell which ones are artifacts and which ones are just rocks. But every now and then he might dig up a rock and mistake it for an artifact."

"So what keeps me from making the same mistake about the whole world? I think the world is an artifact, but maybe it's just a rock. I think it was made by a *who*, but maybe it was caused by a *what*."

"Go back to the principle of sufficient reason."

"Anything that doesn't have to be requires a cause. Right, we said that. But I don't *know* what the—"

"That's only half of the principle."

"There's *another* half?"

"Anything that doesn't have to be requires a cause *sufficient to account for the effect*. Remember the puddle and the picture?"

"Sure."

"The rain could have made the puddle, and the artist could have made the picture, but the rain couldn't have made the picture. That cause wouldn't have been sufficient to account for the effect."

"All right, I can see that the rain couldn't cause a picture. But without knowing all the different kinds of *what* there are, how do I know that there isn't a single *what* that could have been sufficient to cause the world?"

"Think of it this way. Would you agree that the world has both *whos* and *whats* in it?"

"That's pretty obvious."

"And would you also agree that a *who* is greater than a *what*?"

"What do you mean?"

"For one thing, a *what* can make a *what*, and a *who* can make a *what*, but only a *who* can make a *who*."

"That seems true."

"Now put those two points together. If only a *who* can make a *who*, and the world includes *whos*, then only a *who* could make the world."

Peter's eyes widened. "So when I was a kid . . . and I asked *who* made the world—"

"Go on," I said.

"—I was asking the right question."

"You were. You knew intuitively that a powerful *who* was responsible. What you didn't know was *who He was*."

We were silent for a few moments. Then Peter asked, "Why doesn't everyone know this stuff?"

"Deep down," I said, "I think everyone does. It's like what a great teacher of my faith wrote in a letter to one of the early churches: 'For since the creation of the world God's invisible qualities—his eternal power and divine nature—have been clearly seen, *being understood from what has been made,* so that men are without excuse.'"[1]

Peter frowned. "Without excuse for what?"

I smiled. "For pretending they don't know what even a child can see."

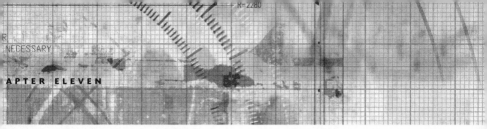

THE WORD WARS

THE ATTITUDE IN HIGHER EDUCATION IS AS SIMPLE AS ABC: ANYTHING BUT CHRISTIANITY.

I'd returned some examinations to my eight o'clock class, and students had lined up outside my door all morning to talk about them. The last student had just left (or so I thought), and I was rising from my desk when a voice from the door arrested me. "Professor Theophilus?" Turning, I saw Mark and Sarah. Mark said, "I was coming over to talk with you, and I bumped into Sarah and discovered that she's irritated by the same thing I am. So I invited her to come along."

"Hi, Professor."

"Hi, people. Have a seat." They refused coffee, so I warmed up my own mug from the pot in the corner of the desk and sat down again. "What are you irritated about? Me?"

"No, we were just hoping you'd have some ideas. Around this campus, every point of view gets heard but one. Sarah and I have both been trying to get a little air time for Christianity."

"Air time?"

"Not radio or TV. I just mean we speak up."

"Good. So what's the problem?"

Sarah said, "Sometimes people listen, and we have a give and take. But other times, the second we open our mouths someone says we're intolerant."

"For instance?"

"Last week some friends and I were talking about abortion. When I said it's wrong, they called me intolerant because I 'didn't respect a woman's choice.'"

Mark chimed in. "Same with my Comparative Religion professor. I didn't agree that there are many roads to God, and he called me intolerant for that."

I took a sip of my coffee. "So are you?" I asked.

"Am I what?"

"Intolerant."

Mark stared at me. "No!" he said.

"I don't think I am either," said Sarah. "But I have to confess that I don't know what tolerance is anymore."

"So what's your question?" I asked.

"What *is* tolerance?" she asked.

"With me it's different," Mark said. "I want to know what to *do* when someone says I'm intolerant. But you can begin with Sarah." She smiled.

"Beginning with Sarah is not only more gentlemanly but also more logical," I explained. "To know what to make of an accusation that you aren't practicing tolerance, you first have to know what it is."

"So what is it?" asked Mark.

"Tell me the word's root."

"The root? I guess *tolerate*."

"Right. What does it mean to tolerate?"

"To put up with something bad."

"Right again."

"So tolerance is . . . putting up with bad things?"

"Depends," I said. "We call tolerance a virtue. Would you call it virtuous to put up with any bad thing—even murder and rape?"

Sarah said, "No, I'd call it stupid and cruel."

"But tolerance couldn't be about putting up with *good* things," said Mark. "So it *must* be about putting up with bad things."

"Sure," I replied. "But not *every* bad thing. Tolerance is the wisdom to know which bad things to put up with and when, why, and to what degree to put up with them—and the settled disposition of acting on that wisdom."

As I took another sip of coffee, Sarah spoke again. "Why put up with *anything* bad?"

"Maybe," said Mark, "because if you didn't, something worse would happen?"

"I don't get it," she answered.

"I mean, for instance, atheism is bad, but what good would it do to pass a law against it? Atheists would just lie and say they were believers. It's better to be an honest atheist than a lying one."

"Right," I agreed. "As Roger Williams said, the sword breeds a nation of hypocrites.[1] Can you think of another example of putting up with a bad thing because otherwise something worse would happen?"

"I get it now," said Sarah. "The repeal of Prohibition. Drunkenness is bad, but a lot of people thought Prohibition encouraged organized crime."

"Freedom of speech," said Mark. "False opinions are bad, but in order to discover the true ones we have to allow debate."

"Jackets," said Sarah.

Mark and I looked blankly at her. "Jackets?"

"Sorry," she said, laughing. "One winter when I was thirteen, I gave my mom a hard time about putting on my jacket. Dad told her to leave me alone, otherwise I'd never learn my lesson for myself."

"Did you learn it?"

"I sure did! It was only twenty degrees outside. I shivered for five minutes, then came in and put on my coat."

Mark chortled, then turned serious again. "Professor T, I get the *which* and *why* parts of your definition, but what about the *when* and *to what degree?*"

"Let's start with *to what degree.* I have a few questions for you. How should we treat a person who acts heroically?"

"A hero? Give him a medal, I guess."

"How about someone who enjoys belching loudly?"

"Are you serious? Avoid him."

"How about a bad-tempered bully who likes to pick fights?"

"Avoid him—and warn others to avoid him too."

"How about a fellow who burglarizes your house?"

"Put him in jail."

"See? For four behaviors, you assigned four different levels of toleration, with honors at one end and punishment at the other. You need the wisdom to know not only what to tolerate, but also how far to go."

Sarah spoke again. "That takes care of *to what degree*. How about *when?*"

"It might be right to put up with something on one occasion but not on another, depending on the circumstances or on how the 'something' is done."

"For instance?"

"Speech. You should put up with people expressing false opinions in debates—"

"I get it. But not with people shouting, 'Fire!' in crowded theaters."

"Right."

"That takes us back to the beginning," she said. "When Mark and I speak from a Christian perspective, some people call us intolerant. Aren't *they* intolerant for trying to shut us up?"

"Sure," I said, "but don't expect them to see it that way. A lot of people simply *define* the Christian view of things as intolerant."

"That's what I mean! First we're told it's intolerant to have strong convictions—"

Mark cut in. "Then we're told it's intolerant to say that anyone else's view is false or that any behavior is wrong."

Sarah again. "Or to express a moral judgment."

"Calm down, crew," I said. "Here are four ground rules. First, it's not necessarily intolerant to express strong convictions."

"All right!" said Sarah.

"But tolerance requires doing so with gentleness and humility. Do you always do that?"

"I could probably do better," she admitted. "Sometimes I just blurt out my convictions without giving my reasons."

I continued. "Second, it's not necessarily intolerant to suggest that an opposing view is false."

"Right on!" said Mark.

"But tolerance requires doing so with charity and patience. Do you always do that?"

"Well, maybe not every single time. I could listen better."

"Third, it's not necessarily intolerant to suggest that a particular behavior should *not* be tolerated."

"Here comes the 'but,'" said Sarah.

"But tolerance requires learning to draw the line."

"What do you mean, Prof?" asked Mark.

"Consider this," I said. "If tolerance is the wisdom of knowing which bad things to put up with, then you can miss the mark in either of two directions, can't you?"

"Two directions?"

"Sure. By putting up with what you shouldn't or by not putting up with what you should."

"Okay, that makes sense."

"What's the fourth ground rule?" asked Sarah.

"It's not necessarily intolerant to express a moral judgment—a conclusion of reasoning about right and wrong or good and bad."

"But?"

"But tolerance requires doing so without presumption or self-righteousness." I finished my coffee and glanced disapprovingly at the empty mug. "Sarah, did I answer the question you came in with?"

"Ye-e-s," she drawled. "But I bet I'll think of more later."

"If you do, let me know," I said. "I'd better get back to work."

"Wait a minute!" protested Mark. "You didn't answer *my* question! I need to know how to *answer* when I'm wrongly accused of intolerance!"

"I can't tolerate another minute of such stimulating conversation," I grinned. "We'll have to talk about that some other time."

THE BIG STORY

POSTMODERNISM AS VIEWED BY A PREMODERNIST.

"Hi, Professor Theophilus — oh, your coffee! I didn't mean to startle you."

"My fault, Sarah. I didn't know you were there. Hand me that spill towel, would you? Right behind you on the hook."

"Sure," she said, complying. "I've never known a professor who kept a spill towel in his office. Is it always that easy to sneak up on you?"

"Yes. It's a good thing I'm not a Renaissance prince. I'd be easy prey for assassins." I tried to keep the coffee from running off the desk onto the floor. "Perhaps you're planning a little assassination yourself this morning?"

"No!"

"Sure about that? No grading complaints, no protests that my shoes are made of leather?"

"None whatsoever, Professor T. I was just hoping you could explain something that's puzzling me in two of my other courses."

"The same thing is puzzling you in both of them?"

"Yes."

"What two courses?"

"Literature and social theory."

Carefully, I encircled the puddle of coffee with the towel. "Have you tried getting help from your professors?"

"Yes, but my literature professor won't tell me his office hours. When I ask for them, he frowns, grumbles something about hegemonic chronologies, and walks away."

"And the social theory professor?"

"She tries to answer my questions, but her answers make me more confused than ever."

"Have you told her that?"

"Yes, and she said, 'It's all part of increasing your negative capacity.'"

I opened my towel drawer, threw the soiled towel in with the others, and stood and hung out a fresh one. Sarah's eyes became a little rounder, but she said nothing. "All right," I said, "tell me what's confusing you in these courses."

"Postmodernism. Both teachers are postmodernists."

"Ahhhhh. Yes, I can see why asking them questions didn't help."

"Can you help me?"

"Maybe. Be more specific."

"Can—you—help—me—understand—postmodernism?"

"No, no. I meant be specific about what's confusing you."

"Well . . ." Sarah pondered. "My lit professor keeps talking about how 'the text does not exist.' At first I thought he meant that we're using a reading packet instead of a textbook, but that's not it."

"Go on."

"He also likes to say, 'We are all perspectivists now.' One day in class I asked, 'Do you just mean that we all have different perspectives on things?' He said, 'Yes! Yes!' So I said, 'I get it. To see how things *really* are we need to *compare* our perspectives, right? And that's why we read literature?'"

"What did he say?"

"Nothing. He slapped his hand to his cheek, rolled his eyes, and said something about Philistines. I knew I'd crashed, but I couldn't figure out why."

I smiled. "And in your social theory course?"

"Now that's really strange," said Sarah. "My social theory teacher keeps talking about 'constructing reality.' I asked, 'Do you mean something like building a civilization?' She answered, 'No, that project belongs to *your* reality.' So I asked, 'What do you mean by *my* reality? How could there be more than one? Do you mean my *interpretation* of reality?'"

"And how did she answer that?"

"She looked owlish and said, 'Listen closely: There is no reality. Interpretation is all there is.'"

"Anything else?"

"Lots and lots. For example, I'm supposed to be 'suspicious of meta-narratives,' whatever *they* are. *Both* of my teachers say that. Oh, Professor T, do you think I'll ever understand postmodernism?"

I laughed. "I think you understand postmodernism very well. The only thing that surprises me is that you haven't come across it on campus before now. Postmodernism is everywhere. It's one of the main ideologies in the modern university."

"But it all sounds like nonsense!"

"It *is* nonsense."

"Oh," she said and was silent for a bit. Then she looked up. "So I'm not stupid?"

"Sarah, your only problem is that you have a little too much common sense."

She chewed on that for a while. "That's nice, Prof, but it doesn't help me out in my two courses."

"No, I shouldn't think it would."

"Do you see my problem? I mean, postmodernism might be nonsense, but it's my *teachers'* nonsense. So knowing that it's nonsense isn't enough. I've got to know what *kind* of nonsense it is, why *they* believe it, and how to *answer* it."

"Well said."

"So?"

"So," I echoed.

"So can you help me?"

I collected my thoughts. "All right, think carefully. *Post* means 'after.' You've taken the European History course. What do you suppose is the *modernism* that *post*modernism is *post?* What big intellectual movement does it come after?"

"Um . . . the Enlightenment, maybe?"

"That will do. And what would you say the Enlightenment was all about?"

"I wrote an essay on that. I'd say it was a time when the intellectual people were trying to make God less important. Am I on the right track?"

"Go on."

"Before the Enlightenment, the intellectuals based their thinking on the Bible. You know — God made man, man rebelled and messed up, God took steps to rescue fallen man — all that."

"Keep going."

"The intellectuals of the Enlightenment tried to see the world as though . . . as though it just didn't make any *difference* whether those things happened. They thought they could figure out Truth without God. No, that's not right. Some of them still believed in an abstract sort of God. But they thought they could figure out Truth without knowing what God had *done*, without . . . without . . ."

"Yes?"

"I was going to say, 'without getting the Big Story right,' but I didn't think it sounded very smart."

"Sarah, it sounds very smart indeed; my grad students couldn't have put it better. Now, how did all that end?"

Sarah reddened. "I don't know, Professor T. My European History course ended in the nineteenth century."

I laughed. "How was it all *starting* to end, then?"

"Well, a lot of intellectuals were still optimistic about finding Truth without getting the Big Story right. But others said this wasn't working."

"Do *you* think it was working?"

"No. If it was, they should have agreed with each other more and more."

"Did they?"

"No. They agreed with each other less and less. About everything. What man is, what life means, how to live — the works."

"If you understand that much, then you'll understand what happened next."

"What?"

"A movement arose that claimed that we *can't* find truth without getting the Big Story right."

"Oh, good."

"Now, you'd think they'd be determined to get the Big Story right, wouldn't you?"

"Sure. Maybe even go back to Revelation — you know, the Bible and all that."

"But here's the catch: Their deepest conviction is that *no one ever* gets the Big Story right. In fact they believe that there isn't any Big Story to *get* right. As the bumper stickers say in cruder language, 'Stuff happens.' That's all."

"And that's postmodernism?"

"Pretty much. For example, take the slogan that you mentioned, 'suspicion of metanarratives.' The word *metanarrative* is just fancy talk for 'Big Story.' So when someone says he's suspicious of metanarratives, he's just saying that no one ever gets the Big Story right."

"But Professor Theophilus — I get that in a way — I mean, now I understand what my teachers are talking about — but it's hypocritical!"

"Why?"

"Because if that's what postmodernism is, then postmodernism itself is a metanarrative! The postmodernists don't practice what they preach. They're only suspicious of everyone *else's* Big Story!"

"Just what do you say their Big Story is?"

"Something like this: 'Once upon a time people believed there was a Big Story that would make sense of things if only they could get it right. Now we know better. There isn't any Big Story, so no one gets it right.'"

"And what do you think of this Big Story?"

"Not much! How can anyone respect a Big Story that lies and pretends that it isn't a Big Story? I'd rather stick with a Big Story that admits it's a Big Story—like 'Creation, Fall, Redemption.'"

"I'm with you," I said, smiling. "Do you feel equipped now to return to the readings in your other courses and figure out what they're all about? You said you needed to find out what kind of nonsense postmodernism is, why postmodernists believe it, and how to answer it. Are you ready to get started?"

"I think so," she said. "I'm going to study the assignments all over again."

"Good, but I want you to remember something. There *is* a grain of truth in postmodernism. Postmodernism thinks that everything is in pieces, that nothing hangs together. The grain of Truth is that without Jesus Christ, everything *does* go to pieces, nothing *does* hang together— not Truth, not life, not anything. You can't fight storylessness with Story unless you remember that He's what makes the Story true."

"Thanks," she said. "I'll remember."

THE WORSHIP MALL

FOR SOME PEOPLE, THE CHURCH IS A CONSUMER PRODUCT.

I had a few moments' warning of her approach because of the rapid *clop-clop-clop* from the hallway. She rounded the curve like a base runner and skidded into my office, coming to a stop just before hitting the file cabinet. Classic Julie. "Sorry, Professor Theophilus," she panted. "I was trying to get here before you left. Your office hours—"

"—don't end for thirty minutes. Why don't you get some running shoes?"

She looked at her feet. "Why, do my sandals look funny?"

"Never mind. Sit down."

She pulled her backpack over her shoulders the way I remove a sweatshirt. Of course it turned over. Books and papers, a compact, a hairbrush, a handkerchief, a couple of apples, and a half-dozen pens and markers spilled everywhere. "Sit *down*, Julie."

"Sorry, sorry!" She dropped cross-legged onto the floor and began scooping things into the backpack. "It's not about school. It's about Zack. I wanted your advice. He—"

"I thought Zack had graduated."

"He did, but he was admitted into the MA program."

"I thought he'd decided he didn't need an MA."

"He had, but he's changed his career plan." She beamed. "That's fine with me because he's doing his MA here."

"Has he—?"

"Not yet, but I think he's going to." She glanced up. "When I said I had a problem with Zack, did you think I meant a *romantic* problem?"

"The thought had crossed my mind."

"Ha ha! No, it's a religious problem. An *ecclesial* . . . an *ecclesiolastical*—"

"Ecclesiological?"

"Right. About churches. That's why I thought I should ask you. You know about things like that." She zipped her backpack, rose, and sat down in a regular chair.

"Julie, I dislike opining about where-to-go-to-church problems almost as much as opining about what-to-do-with-boyfriend problems."

"Oh, you won't mind hearing about *this* where-to-go-to-church problem. It'll interest you. See, Zack goes to the Eclipsitarian church. The one over on the north side of campus."

"I know the one."

"It's way different than what I'm used to. I grew up in independent churches. The Eclipsitarians are a real, you know, denomination."

"Mmm hmm."

"But I don't have a problem with that."

"Of course not."

"Did I mention the prayers? They have set prayers. Everyone says the same words, all at the same time. Just like they're singing a praise song, except they're not singing. Zack said, 'If you can have set words for songs, then why can't you have set words for prayers?' I said, 'Because they're completely different, silly. Those are songs; these are prayers.'"

"Mmm hmm."

"It's so weird. But I don't have a problem with that either."

"Perish the thought."

"Speaking of praise songs, they sing theirs in a strange way. Not with the words projected on the wall, like in regular churches. Out of books instead."

"Mmm hmm."

"But I don't even have a problem with *that*."

"Commendably broad-minded."

"Thanks. The problem is this: See, they used to believe in the Bible. Zack and the other people in his church still do. They say that traditionally, Eclipsitarians have been very biblical."

"Why is that a problem?"

"It's not. The problem is that they *don't* believe in the Bible anymore."

"I thought you said they did."

"I said that the people in Zack's *own* church do. But in lots of Eclipsitarian churches, they don't. Not really. They still read the Bible on Sunday, but they pick and choose what teachings to believe."

"How have you learned all this?"

"Zack told me. There was a big Eclipsitarian convention. A national meeting. A pastor was there who had deserted his wife and children to live with his homosexual partner. And instead of telling him he couldn't be a pastor anymore, they made him a bishop or pope or something. You won't tell me *that's* biblical."

"No, of course not."

"Lots of other awful things were done. For instance, they made a rule that churches could bless same-sex unions if they wanted to. I heard a spokesman for the denomination on television. He said something like, 'If the Bible, Christian tradition, and two thousand years of consistent teaching are against this, then the Bible, Christian tradition, and two thousand years of consistent teaching are wrong.'[1] I'm surprised you haven't heard about any of these things."

"I have heard about them. I have Eclipsitarian friends, and they're in agony. They're watching their denomination destroy itself."

"Oh! Then you'll understand what I told Zack."

"What did you tell him?"

"That he should leave a denomination like that. If it isn't biblical anymore, he should get out of it."

"What did Zack say?"

"He said he's not sure. He talked about a faithful remnant and said maybe some people should stay and fight. Professor T, how can I show him he's wrong?"

"What do you want him to do, Julie?"

"He should do like I do. I won't worship where they don't believe the Bible."

"Where do you worship?"

"Oh, *lots* of places." I raised an eyebrow. She began ticking them off on her fingers. "On Christmas I went with some friends to the Pretzelterian church out on First Street because it's so pretty with all the lights. On Easter I went to University Whatever Church because they did a passion play. When I'm feeling low, I go to the Church of the Gladfest. When I want to hear good music, I go to the Church of the Frozen. When I want to meet friendly people, I go to the Church of the Thawed. At least once a month I go to Sam 'n Alice's Independent Bible Church because the preaching is good and it reminds me of what I grew up with. And last Sunday," she finished triumphantly, "I went to MacChurch because they have a *great* college ministry."

"Let me rephrase my question. To what congregation do you *belong*?"

"Belong?"

"You've only told me some churches that you visit."

"When you say, 'belong,' do you mean like on a membership roll?"

I smiled. "For starters."

"Well, nowhere. The Bible doesn't say anything about membership rolls."

I collected my thoughts before speaking. "Julie," I said, "I don't presume to know whether God's will for Zack is to stay and fight. I only know that *if* he stays, then he has no godly option but to fight. As for you, if you really want my advice—"

"I do!"

"Then I advise you to stay out of it. You have nothing to teach him in this matter. Don't make his decision more difficult by imagining that you do."

She was stunned. "What do you mean?"

"I mean that Zack is trying to decide his duty to God regarding the Church. You don't yet believe in the Church."

"Of course I believe in going to church!"

"That's just it. You believe in *going to* church, but you don't believe in *Church*. You can *go to* a football game or a shopping mall — or for that matter a passion play — but Church isn't something you *go to*. It's the family of God, the Body of Christ, the outpost of heaven. You belong to it as you belong to your birth family. You grow into it as your limbs grow into your physical body. You are taken into it as you are taken into the life of the Holy Spirit."

"I thought that I belonged to God's family just by being born again."

"You do — like a child belongs to his earthly family just by being born physically. But when you treat Church as a worship mall, you're forgetting everything you know about earthly families."

"What do you mean?"

"The members of a family are parts of a larger whole. They share in a common life and bear each others' joys and burdens. If that's what even earthly family is all about, how much more the family of God! Christ has been taking care of you the way parents take care of their baby. But He wants you to grow up into your inheritance."

For a few moments Julie was silent. Then she said, "I haven't the foggiest idea what you're talking about."

I grinned. "Talk to Zack."

FAITH ON CAMPUS LETTERS

ABSOLUTELY CONFUSED

Dear Professor Theophilus:

It is all well and good to talk about moral absolutes. Logically and biblically they must exist. However, the average person who does not believe in moral absolutes always wants me to name one, and I find it difficult to name one that satisfies him. The typical example of "Don't kill" invites the questions, "What about war?," "What about capital punishment?," "What about self-defense or the defense of others?," and "What if it was Hitler?" I guess my question is this: Can you state a moral assertion that satisfies a person who is looking for an absolute?

Reply: The reason you're getting in trouble with "Don't kill" is that the more accurate translation is "Don't murder." Murder isn't simply taking life; it's directly or deliberately taking innocent human life (and even taking *guilty* human life is murder if you aren't the one with the authority to take it). There are no exceptions to the prohibition of murder, so if by a moral absolute you mean a moral rule to which there are no exceptions, then the prohibition of murder is certainly one of them. Frankly, absolutes are easy to find. Some others are "Do not commit adultery," "Do not fornicate," "Honor your parents," "Love God," and "Love your neighbor." None of these have exceptions. If they will satisfy your friends is another matter. That depends on whether they are looking for truth or excuses!

Grace and peace,
Professor Theophilus

WHAT'S THE BIG DEAL? (OR WHY ARE THESE DEALS BIGGER?)

Dear Professor Theophilus:

It seems that sexual sins (like premarital sex, adultery, and pornography) and murder (like abortion, suicide, and assisted suicide) are more strongly condemned than other sins. Why is it that of all the sins that mankind can think to commit, these two in particular bear such a stigma? Why aren't lying or stealing or cheating equally bad? I know that sin is sin and that no matter how big or small some particular sins might seem to us mere humans, they all separate us from God. So what's the big deal about sexual sins and murder? I thought maybe there might be some sort of connection between the two that you might explain.

Reply: Good questions! I won't comment on whether murder and the misuse of the sexual powers are the most sinful of all, and I don't want to lessen the gravity of other sins, but these two are certainly grave and the reasons deserve explanation. Let's start with murder.

Murder is heinous primarily because of what it destroys. It isn't like stealing. You see, money is only money, but man is the image of God. To murder a man is to desecrate God's image and thereby to insult God Himself. Another reason murder is so terrible is that it is irreparable. You can give money back, but you can't give back a life. Finally, murder hurts so many people. Not without reason are weapons of violence called "widow makers." They might with equal justice be called "orphan makers," "debt makers," and "makers of despair."

Sexual immorality is also an insult to the image of God. Genesis 1:27 says, "So God created man in his own image, in the image of God he created him; male and female he created them." Do you get the picture? It is not only man and woman individually, but man and woman *together* that make the image of God; the love of the spouses images the love of the Father, Son, and Holy Spirit. It follows that to deface the relationship between man and woman is to deface God's image in humanity. Related to this is another great "mystery" of the faith: Paul says in Ephesians 5 that the relation of husband and wife represents to us the relation of Christ and the Church, His bride. Sexual immorality defaces that image too.

Another reason why sexual immorality is so gravely wrong is that, like murder, it hurts so many people. The rightly-ordered love of husband and wife is the seed of the family, but wrongly-ordered sexual passion ruins families, twists families, and prevents families from forming. And let's not forget that in the end, sexual immorality actually *generates* murder. Why do we have such an epidemic of abortions? Because people want to have sex yet reject the divine gift of children.

Speaking for myself, I hadn't originally planned to spend so much time in my columns addressing sexual matters. What changed my mind was my mail from readers. The letters dramatized that the sexual disorder of our time is wreaking havoc among Christians too—much more than I thought. People are in misery. Perhaps in another day and age it would be more important to talk about different sins, but this is the age that we live in.

Grace and peace,
Professor Theophilus

IT DOESN'T HURT ANYONE

Dear Professor Theophilus:

I stand on the fact that God ultimately defines what is right and wrong. But my friend bases his entire moral code upon the idea that "as long as I am not directly hurting anyone other than me, then nothing that I do is wrong." I don't have an intelligent response. Do you?

Reply: C. S. Lewis once remarked that the inventors of "new moralities" don't really invent new moralities; they merely accept the bits of the old morality that they like and ignore the bits of the old morality that they don't like.[1] For example, an extreme Nationalist accepts the parts about our duty to kin but ignores the parts about all men being brothers, and an extreme Socialist accepts the parts about our duty to relieve suffering but ignores the parts about justice and good faith. Your friend is doing much the same thing, for the duty to avoid unnecessary harm to others is a genuine part of the moral law. His problem isn't that it's wrong; his problem is that he ignores all the other parts.

The first problem with throwing out every duty but the avoidance of harm to others is that it will make him *flat*. We were made to serve God, not just ourselves. In the words of the Westminster Catechism (these are words that both Protestants and Catholics can accept), "Man's chief and highest end is to glorify God, and fully to enjoy Him forever."[2] By casting aside our greatest duty, your friend is also casting aside our greatest joy and privilege.

The second problem with his way of life is that it will make him *selfish*. What would he think of a man who had never lifted a finger to protect his wife but bragged that he had never beat her? Or a man who failed to sound the fire alarm but boasted that he hadn't set the fire? How about a teacher who had never taught his students an important truth but preened himself on the fact that he had never taught them a lie? Frankly, I don't believe that your friend would admire such people any more than you would. But by claiming that his only duty is to avoid unnecessary harm to others, he is training himself to be just like them.

The third problem with your friend's narrow-mindedness is that it will make him *stupid*. If the only duty he recognizes is not harming others, he won't have the foggiest idea of what harming others means. This is already happening in the way he limits harm to *direct* harm, then limits it even further to "hurt," to *physical* harm. Suppose that through reckless driving I were to get myself killed, leaving my wife a widow. Would the fact that the harm of widowhood was indirect make it small?

ASK ME ANYTHING 117

Suppose that I were to corrupt a young female student by seducing her. Would the fact that the harm of corruption was nonphysical make it trivial? You see, every moral duty depends on the other moral duties to flesh it out and complete its meaning. By keeping one duty but throwing out the others, your friend eventually won't even understand the one that he keeps.

The slogan, "It can't be wrong if it doesn't hurt anyone" first became popular as a rationalization for sex outside of marriage. That was thirty-five years ago. Now, after tens of millions of abortions, divorces, father-less children, sterilization-inducing diseases, and broken hearts, perhaps it's time to reconsider the meaning of *hurt*. I don't know what your friend hopes to justify, but you can be sure he is looking for a way to justify something he really knows is wrong.

Just so you don't overlook it: We've been talking about the surface issue—your friend's claim to be ignorant of every moral duty but avoiding harm to others. But there is a deeper issue—his implicit claim to be ignorant of his moral and spiritual dependence on God. That's where he most needs your prayer.

Grace and peace,
Professor Theophilus

RIGHT BACK ON THE HOOK

Dear Professor Theophilus:

You wrote to one guy that a certain Old Testament rule about punishments "does not apply to our society because it was a Hebrew civil regulation, not a universal moral law." My question is this: How does one distinguish between ancient "civil regulations" and laws that still apply today? Also, why are so many regulations that don't apply to us included in the Bible? What is the purpose of their inclusion?

Reply: The short answer is that all of the *moral* principles underlying Torah, or Old Testament law, still apply to us, including all of the Ten Commandments. But not everything in Torah applies to us. The regulations that don't apply include the following:

1. The *ceremonial* regulations, for example how the priest must dress.
2. The *dietary* regulations, for example the prohibition of eating pork.
3. The regulations for *ritual purity*, for example the special rules for women during their menstrual periods.
4. The *sacrificial* regulations, for example when to sacrifice a lamb and when to sacrifice a goat.
5. The *civil* regulations that establish judicial procedures and legal penalties, for example what should be done when one man causes injury to another.

The rule my other reader asked about was in category five, so let's zero in on Old Testament civil regulations. First, why *don't* they apply to us? One reason is that the kinds of social arrangements people need vary according to circumstances in a way that moral truths do not. For example, striking one's neighbor is wrong everywhere, but it doesn't follow that the same punishment for striking one's neighbor is appropriate everywhere. Another reason Hebrew civil regulations don't apply to us is that they were part of a system that no longer exists—a government directly established by God. Only once in history has God ruled a people directly. He did this with the Chosen People because He had set them apart as a "light to the nations"; they were to be the people among whom the Messiah would be born.

The fact that we are released from Old Testament civil penalties doesn't mean that we are released from their underlying moral purposes. Those still stand, and the passage the other fellow asked about illustrates this point too. It was the regulation in Exodus 22:16 that declares, "If a man seduces a virgin who is not pledged to be married and sleeps with her, he must pay the bride-price, and she shall be his wife." The young man who wrote to me had seduced his girlfriend, but he didn't want to marry her. Could he get off the hook? I told him that he was off *that* hook but still stuck on another one. As I wrote, "You may not be obligated by the Old Testament requirement to marry the girl, but you have taken something from her that you can never give back. You need to repent of your legalistic attitude and give serious and prayerful thought to how you can make that up to her. In the meantime, because both of you have committed a serious sin, both of you must also repent. You say you want to do what God wants, but you don't mention being sorry that you didn't."

In fact, God had special purposes for the Hebrews in *every* category of regulation. In some cases we have a pretty good idea what these special purposes were and in other cases we don't. For example, the sacrificial regulations anticipated and symbolized the future sacrifice of Christ upon the cross. Because of what He did, we no longer need a sacrament of atonement yet to come; instead, we need a sacrament of the atonement already accomplished. That's why Christ commanded us to celebrate Holy Communion.

The bottom line is that the *moral* principles of Torah still apply to us—and so do the underlying moral principles of the other regulations. Many of these moral principles have actually been clarified and strengthened for us by Jesus Christ. Consider the "you have heard . . . but I tell you" passages in the Sermon on the Mount (see Matthew 5:21-48).

Grace and peace,
Professor Theophilus

DOES IT DO ANY GOOD TO PRAY?

Dear Professor Theophilus:

What is the purpose of prayer? Can it change God's mind or influence His actions? It seems from the actions of Moses that this is possible. I guess I was wondering more specifically about prayer for unbelievers. I have searched the entire New Testament and have found only one instance of Jesus asking us to pray for our enemies. And in John 17:9, Jesus said that He doesn't pray for the world but for those who will believe in Him. What's your viewpoint on this? Should I pray for my unbelieving friends? Or should I pray just for those who are appointed to salvation? What effect do my prayers have on a God who sees the choices people with free will make?

Reply: Good questions. God teaches us to pray, and even Jesus prayed, though He was perfectly united with the Father. Surely God takes our prayers into account. After all, why would He instruct us to do something useless? It's true that from the depths of his bitterness, Job once wondered whether prayers have any point, but he later confessed that he hadn't realized what he was talking about (see Job 21:15; 42:1-6). Besides, Scripture is full of instances in which God adjusted His plans in accordance with human requests—not just the requests of Moses, but the requests of other biblical figures too. I'd like you to notice that many of these prayers were offered on behalf of other people, including nonbelievers. For example, when Agrippa said to Paul, his prisoner, "Do you think that in such a short time you can persuade me to be a Christian?" Paul replied, "Short time or long—*I pray God* that not only you but all who are listening to me today may become what I am, except for these chains" (Acts 26:28-29, emphasis added).

Yes, I understand that you have found only one command from Jesus to pray for our enemies. By the way, it's recorded in two places: Matthew 5:44 and Luke 6:28. But how many times does Jesus have to say it? Three? Thirty? The Son of God Himself is speaking; isn't once enough? And how could we pray just for those whom God knows will be saved? He hasn't told us who they are.

You end with a good question—how *could* our prayers affect a God who sees the choices people with free will make? There are various theories about this, but one point may help. Yes, God's knowledge is eternal. But remember, He eternally knows more than one thing. From eternity He knows how nonbelievers respond to His actions toward them, but from eternity He also knows what prayers their Christian friends offer on their behalf. There is no reason why He cannot, from eternity, adjust His actions toward nonbelievers according to the prayers that He accepts. Does that help?

Of course, we don't know from experience what that's like because we know things successively—moment by moment—rather than all at once like Him. But we don't have to know what it's like to know that He can do it.

Grace and peace,
Professor Theophilus

WHY DOESN'T GOD SEEM TO HELP?

Dear Professor Theophilus:

I'm confused about something. How closely is God involved with each of us? I mean, if you take someone with a drinking problem (or porn, drugs, whatever) and he really wants to quit, why do you suppose God doesn't help right away? Here is someone really reaching out, and it seems as if the help is not provided because he still remains hooked. Those that do quit seem to quit because of their own will. Please respond. Thanks.

Reply: You raise good questions. How deeply does God really care for us? He loves us more than we can imagine. But if that's true, then when an addicted person wants to quit, why doesn't God help right away? Don't those who do quit do so of their own free will?

Sometimes the best answer to a question is another question. How do you know God *doesn't* help right away? I would say that He *must* be helping. Addiction weakens our free will. If an addicted person is nevertheless able to quit of his own free will—something that would seem to be impossible—why not say instead that Christ is giving help to his free will?

You see, God gave free will to us. It's His gift. His idea of healing us isn't to override the gift but to make the gift holy. He could have made us robots without free will—beings that made no real decisions but did the right thing no matter what. Some people would like that because then there wouldn't be such things as addiction; we'd escape the very possibility of self-inflicted evils. Here's the problem with that so-called solution: Without free will, we would also escape the possibility of the greatest goods. How so? You see, God loves us, and it was His purpose to make us in His own image—little finite copies of Himself, able to receive His love and to love Him in return. But for that, free will is crucial. No robot can love because love, by its nature, is something freely chosen.

Do you see how this works? To be made in His image we must be capable of love; to be capable of love we must have free will; but to have free will, we must also be capable of willing wrongly. To "fix" the addicted person by *destroying* his already-weakened free will would be to complete his destruction. It would also make all his decisions meaningless because they wouldn't really be his.

Instead, in Christ, God does something much more amazing, much more profound, something that transcends our understanding. Rather than destroying our free will, He heals it.

But what about those who *don't* escape their addiction? Isn't God helping them? There are three issues here.

First, you say the person "really wants to quit." How do you know that? When we are wrapped up in our sins, we often say to other people that we want to quit, even though we don't really. We even try to convince ourselves of the lie. Only Christ can penetrate the veil of deceptions and self-deceptions; we can't.

Second, although you say that the person wants to quit, you don't say that the person wants God's help in quitting. God doesn't often help without our asking. Often we don't even want His help. To receive His help is to give up control, to abandon the claim of self-ownership, to admit that we are in ruins and cannot help ourselves. This is a blow to our sinful pride. Besides, it is a fearsome thing to pass our sins into the hands of the living God—even into His helping hands—for God's idea of helping may be quite different from our own. Our idea of help may be merely that we escape some sin or addiction and then return to our old lives, still without Him. But His love is inexorable, and in the torrent of that love He desires goods for us that we have never thought of and that would, in our present state, make us tremble to conceive.

Third, although God will one day wipe every tear from the eyes of His redeemed, He does not promise to heal every hurt in *this* life. Every now and then we get glimpses of some of the reasons. Here's what Paul wrote about one of his own afflictions:

> *To keep me from becoming conceited because of these surpass-ingly great revelations, there was given me a thorn in my flesh, a messenger of Satan, to torment me. Three times I pleaded with the Lord to take it away from me. But he said to me, "My grace is sufficient for you, for my power is made perfect in weakness." Therefore I will boast all the more gladly about my weaknesses, so that Christ's power may rest on me. That is why, for Christ's sake, I delight in weaknesses, in insults, in hardships, in perse-cutions, in difficulties. For when I am weak, then I am strong.* (2 Corinthians 12:7-10)

The triune God made us for Himself, and He will be satisfied with nothing less than our transformation, purifying and burnishing us until we reflect back His image as perfectly as the angels reflect His light. Do we want that much help, that much good, that much glory? That is the question.

Grace and peace,
Professor Theophilus

DEARGODI'MSORRYFORALLMYSINSAMEN

Dear Professor Theophilus:

Can we repent of all our sins at once, or does each have to be repented of separately?

Reply: If you had committed numerous wrongs against your girlfriend, how would you apologize to her? Would you say, "Sorry for everything, babe, now let's get on with it"? Or would you say, "I'm sorry for doing *this*, and *this*, and *this*, and *this*, and *this*. The memory of how I've hurt you is intolerable. Can you find the mercy to forgive me?" It isn't that she couldn't possibly forgive you the first way—I suppose you *might* mean it—but the second way is better for your relationship and for you. So it is between us and God.

Grace and peace,
Professor Theophilus

PROFESSOR PAGAN

Dear Professor Theophilus:

I attend a Christian college and plan to be a missionary. During the break I'm taking a cultural anthropology class at the local community college so that I can transfer the credit to my own school later. The problem is that although the professor is kind toward other religions, he is harsh and vulgar toward Christianity, and I'm not sure how to respond. He says things like, "There are no true religions;" "Did God create us or did we create God?;" and "Missionaries force their religious beliefs down the throats of others at all costs."

To defend his hostility toward missionaries, he offers the relativistic proposition that "every culture has value and should be judged by its own standards." Of course I don't think that missionaries should go into other lands to undermine their cultures! If my cross-cultural classes in my missions studies have taught me anything, it's that the gospel must be contextualized so that each cultural group can clearly understand Christ's sacrifice.

I also need a Christian perspective on dinosaurs and fossil records. My professor has claimed that the first signs of human life appeared about four million years ago. Does the Bible really say that humans have only been in existence for about six thousand years, as my professor claims? If so, then how am I to deal with physical evidence like carbon dating that seems to undermine the historical record of Scripture?

As you can see, I am frustrated and confused. Thank you very much!

Reply: Your professor is all too typical, and I'm glad you've written. I gather that you have five main questions for me: (1) How can you respond to his strange declarations about subjects like religious truth and cultural relativity? (2) How can you respond to his ignorant and bigoted remarks about Christian missionaries? (3) Does the Bible really claim that the first human beings appeared only about six thousand years ago? (4) Whatever the answer to the previous question, how can you respond when your professor begins spouting off about Genesis? (5) What is the right approach to take to his question, "Did God create us or did we create God?" Let's take these questions in turn.

As to the first question, I think you should "play back the tape" to your professor. In other words, turn his own claims back on him, but in the form of questions. When he says, "There are no true religions," you might say something like this—in your own words, of course:

> *I'm interested in your statement that no one possesses religious truth —I guess you mean that no one can justify any theological claim. It puzzles me, though, because your statement is a theological claim. If no one knows the truth about religion, then how can you say that your claim about religion is true?*

Later in the discussion, you might add,

> *You see, it's like the famous Liar's Paradox. A man says, "The statement I am making is a lie." The paradox is that if the*

> *statement is true, then it can't be true because he just said it's a lie; but if the statement is false, then he's lying, but that makes it true after all. Your statement is the same. You say, "No beliefs about religion are true," but that is a belief about religion.*

The same strategy will be helpful when he says, "Every culture has value and should be judged by its own standards." Turn the claim back on him in the form of a question. For example, you might ask this question and watch him squirm:

> *Professor, I'm having a little trouble with the idea that every culture has value and should be judged by its own standards. Do you think that the Nazi culture had value and should be judged by its own standards — so that the better it was at genocide, the more we should approve it?*

Or you might ask the following question, which is a little more abstract:

> *Professor, even from your own point of view, isn't there a certain problem in judging every culture by its own standards? Suppose that culture X believes itself to be superior to all the other cultures and believes that each of those cultures should be judged by culture X's standards. What would it mean to judge that culture by its own standards?*

Here's a variation on the last one:

> *Professor, whose culture says that we ought to judge every culture by its own standards? Isn't it just your culture — the culture of university anthropology teachers? The reason I'm asking is that if that's true, then it seems inconsistent for you to teach that other people accept your standard. Doing that seems*

like judging the surrounding culture not by its own standards,
but by the standards of your culture.

On to your second question: How can you respond to your professor's ignorant and bigoted remarks about Christian missionaries? There are two different ways. One way, of course, is to use the same strategy of "playing back the tape" that I recommended when I answered your first question. On a day when he has been venting his opinions about how nasty Christians are, you might ask him a question like this:

> *I'm trying to understand the idea that every culture has value*
> *and should be judged by its own standards. If that's true, then*
> *doesn't the culture of Christianity also have value, and*
> *shouldn't we judge it by its own standards? In that case I don't*
> *understand why you are so harsh on Christian missionaries.*

The other approach is different. Point out to your teacher that your own missionary training has strongly emphasized the importance of respecting the culture of the host country. Not only that, but the insight that the gospel must be presented in such a way that each cultural group can clearly understand Christ's sacrifice isn't new—it's even biblical! That is precisely how the Bible itself teaches missionaries to present the gospel. Consider how Paul spoke to the pagans in Athens. He began by quoting from *their* poets, and he called attention to *their* altar inscribed "To An Unknown God." If you read Acts 17, you'll see what I mean.

Next, your third question: Does the Bible really claim that the first human beings appeared only about six thousand years ago? The question is whether the inspired authors of the genealogies in the first eleven chapters of Genesis intended them to be taken literally or figuratively. Like the question of whether the six "days" of creation are literal days (24-hour periods) or figurative days (phases of creation), this is one of the few points that serious biblical Christians disagree about, and serious arguments have been offered on both sides. (By the way, serious arguments have also been offered both for and against carbon dating.) All serious biblical Christians agree, however, that some language in the Bible is figurative. Most of my readers are familiar with my favorite example: When the Bible calls Jesus the Lamb of God, it doesn't mean that He has horns, hooves, and a wooly coat, but that He is our sacrifice for sin. Apparently your professor doesn't know much about biblical interpretation.

On to your fourth question: No matter which way the early biblical genealogies are intended, how can you respond when your professor begins spouting off about Genesis? You need to do two things. The first is simply to explain to him what I explained to you in the previous paragraph—that the correct interpretation of the Genesis genealogies is a matter of debate among Christians, so he can't simply say, "The Bible says." The second and more important is to emphasize what both sides of the debate *do* agree about—that no matter how the Genesis genealogies are to be interpreted and no matter how long human beings have been upon the earth, they are here by God's design and plan and nothing in human history can be fully understood apart from His purposes. To put this another way, get your professor off the relatively unimportant points like *how* God brought it about that human beings are on this planet, *when* He brought it about, and whether He brought it about by a gradual process or all at once. Redirect his focus to the more important point of *who* is responsible for the fact that human beings are on this planet. Genesis says that God is responsible.

After you redirect his focus, he may try to beat you over the head with Darwin. I'm sure you know the drill: "As the evidence shows, man is the result of a meaningless and purposeless process that did not have us in mind," and so on and so forth. Actually, the evidence shows nothing of the kind; what it actually suggests is Intelligent Design. To see how Darwinists have distorted the evidence, take a look at the new book *Icons of Evolution* by Jonathan Wells (Regnery Publishing, 2000). To see how the evidence points to Intelligent Design, see any of the books on the subject by Michael Behe, William Dembski, or Phillip Johnson or visit the website of the Center for the Renewal of Science and Culture (www.discovery.org/crsc/). I think you'll be surprised.

Finally, what's wrong with your professor asking, "Did God create us or did we create God?" Considering the variety of completely incompatible religions in the world, I think it's a pretty good question. The only problem is that he left out one of the possible answers! Considering what's written in passages like Romans 1:18-25, you could say something like this:

> *It's interesting that you ask that question because my own faith tradition recognizes the fact of religious diversity just like you do. But our teacher Paul gave a different explanation. He explained that God created us and we "created" gods — false gods — because we don't want to acknowledge the true one. In fact, the Christian idea is that the manufacture of false gods is still going on today. The only difference is that instead of having names like Zeus and Athena, today they have names like Sex, Getting Rich, My Inner Self, and Getting My Way.*

The way this answer works is that it affirms the element of truth in what the other person has said but uses it as a springboard for another truth the other person hasn't recognized. Paul did that all the time. You see what I'm suggesting to you, don't you? Think of your missionary training again. You're "contextualizing" biblical truth so that this pagan can understand it — a pagan who happens to be your teacher.

I think you're going to have to be the kind of missionary your professor doesn't expect. As you pursue your studies, may God illuminate your intellect and show you how to hold your own with courtesy, courage, and persistence.

Grace and peace,
Professor Theophilus

IS IT BAD TO REASON?

Dear Professor Theophilus:

Is philosophical reasoning intrinsically good or bad? As a college student I often hear that reasoning is the best way to understand life. Well, I know that God makes sense, that He works by certain principles, and that we are supposed to know the reasons that we believe instead of going through life blindly. Does this mean that we can reach Christianity through reasoning alone? How do we go about reaching someone who does believe in reasoning alone?

Reply: Reasoning is good in itself. God created our powers of reasoning along with everything else, and at the end of His creation He pronounced what He had made good (see Genesis 1:31). Jesus taught that we are to love the Lord our God not only with all our heart and all our soul and all our strength, but also with all our mind (see Mark 12:30 and Luke 10:27). In Isaiah 1:18, when God desired to teach His wayward people how desperate their condition was, He said, "Come now, let us reason together." In another passage in Isaiah, He challenged those who had departed from His ways to vie with Him in reasoning (see 43:26). When King Nebuchadnezzar's madness ended and his reason returned to him, he praised God (see Daniel 4:36-37). The author of the book of Ecclesiastes was commended because he weighed the traditional sayings or proverbs, and weighing is an exercise of reason (see Ecclesiastes 12:9, RSV). In 1 Corinthians 10:15, Paul challenged the Christians of Corinth to test his words by reasoning: "I speak as to sensible men; judge for yourselves what I say." Peter instructed those who dealt with challengers to reason gently with them: "Always be prepared to make a defense to any one who calls you to account for the hope that is in you, yet do it with gentleness and reverence" (1 Peter 3:15, RSV). When Paul was summoned by Felix, the Roman governor, he reasoned so persuasively about justice, self-control, and future judgment that Felix was unnerved (see Acts 24:25). To demonstrate from the Scriptures that Jesus was the Christ, Paul used reasoned arguments (see Acts 17:2-3; 18:4, 19). Even apart from the Bible, by reasoning from the Creation man recognizes that there is an eternal and powerful Creator (see Romans 1:20).

The problem with reasoning isn't that reason is bad, but that fallen creatures reason badly. Yes, reason alone teaches us that there is a Creator, but from time immemorial people have suppressed this knowledge (see Romans 1:18-19). What the world calls "wisdom" is not true wisdom, and the wisdom of the gospel seems folly to the world (see 1 Corinthians 1:18-29; 2:4-8). Therefore, so-called human wisdom is not sufficient to teach the gospel—our minds need God's grace (see 1 Corinthians 2:13-15). In fact, all too often human wisdom is nothing but a craving for novelty—an itching to hear something new (see Acts 17:21). Against this kind of "philosophy" Paul sternly warned (see Colossians 2:8; 1 Timothy 6:20). If we Christians are to practice philosophy—and I believe that we are—then we must practice it in a different way, "for the weapons of our warfare are not worldly but have divine power to destroy strongholds. We destroy arguments and every proud obstacle to the knowledge of God, and take every thought captive to obey Christ" (2 Corinthians 10:4-5, RSV). Our charter as Christian thinkers is Paul's command in Romans 12:2: "Do not be conformed to this world but be transformed by the renewal of your mind, that you may prove"—that means test—"what is the will of God, what is good and acceptable and perfect" (RSV).

Now, how can we go about reaching people who say they believe in reasoning "alone"? One thing I often do is point out to them that there is no such thing as reasoning alone. Consider this: Could a person prove, by reasoning, that reasoning works? Of course not; any such "proof" would be circular, and as everyone knows, circular reasoning proves nothing. Then how does the reasoner get his confidence in reasoning? He certainly doesn't get it by reasoning alone; he takes the reliability of reasoning on faith. What this shows is that faith is not the *opposite* of reasoning, as silly people often think; rather, faith is necessary to the act of reasoning itself. No one can choose whether or not to have faith; the only choice open to him is where his faith should be placed.

Suppose someone answers this by saying, "Okay, I admit that I have faith in reasoning. But I refuse to have faith in anything *else*; reasoning is the *only* thing in which I'll place my faith." There are two problems with this way of reasoning about reasoning. First, it's arbitrary. Once a person admits that one act of faith is reasonable, on what grounds can he argue that all *other* acts of faith are *un*reasonable? Second, it's shortsighted. The first thing that any honest person learns about his reasoning powers is how limited they are. He can find out some things with them, but he cannot find out the most important things with them. God, who created human reason, must have known this. Therefore, it is *reasonable* to believe that if God wants us to know more about Him than just the fact that He exists, He would have given our reasoning extra help to know the things that it couldn't reach by itself. That's why He has given us biblical revelation.

You see, to know the limits of sight is not to be blind; true blindness lies in refusing extra light when it is offered.

Has this helped? May God bless your reasoning; may He, by the power of the Spirit, so renew your mind that you will indeed be transformed; may He grant you a spirit not only to "prove" but to abide in what is good and acceptable and perfect.

Grace and peace,
Professor Theophilus

FLASH: STUDENT'S PROFESSOR NOT A BELIEVER

Dear Professor Theophilus:

I can relate to the student who asked whether reasoning is good or bad because I, too, am in a philosophy course emphasizing the authority of reason. You affirmed reasoning but pointed out that even reasoning depends on faith—faith that reasoning works. When I mentioned this to my professor, he responded that faith in reason is different from religious faith because faith in reason is testable and religious beliefs aren't. How would you respond?

Reply: Your professor is confusing the question of whether beliefs are testable by reason (many are) with the question of whether the reasoning power itself is testable by reason (it isn't; such a test would be circular and thus worthless). As to whether *religious* beliefs can be tested by reason, he makes a second error when he states categorically that they can't be. Many can be, and the Christian faith actually demands such testing.

For example, Paul, confronted with various wild claims of prophecy, instructed the Thessalonians not to despise prophecy but not to be gullible either: "Test everything. Hold on to the good" (1 Thessalonians 5:21). Similarly, the New Testament authors did not expect the empty tomb and the Resurrection appearances to be believed just because they said so; they cited witnesses and emphasized that many of the witnesses were still alive (implying that they could be questioned). In the same spirit, the book of Acts praises the Bereans for the cautious spirit in which they tested Paul's claims by comparing them with Hebrew scriptures (see 17:10-12). It is sometimes argued that this is not true testing because the standard—Scripture—is itself accepted without test. But it isn't. Everything in Scripture that *can* be independently confirmed proves true; it is reasonable, then, to believe that the things that *cannot* be independently confirmed are true too.

I suspect that your professor is unfamiliar with the extensive Christian literature on the rational grounds for faith. The term for this literature is *apologetics* from the Greek word *apologion*, which means "defense." There are a lot of good books on Christian apologetics, and I think you would get great benefit from looking into them.

Probably your professor wouldn't be interested in reading a book of apologetics, but there is something else you can do with him. Go to the library and get the latest issue of *Faith and Philosophy*—it's the official journal of the Society of Christian Philosophers. Show it to him and ask (with a smile), "Are you trying to tell me that these aren't reasoned arguments?" You see, philosophy of religion just happens to be where the action is in philosophy these days, and the best work is being done by Christians.

Grace and peace,
Professor Theophilus

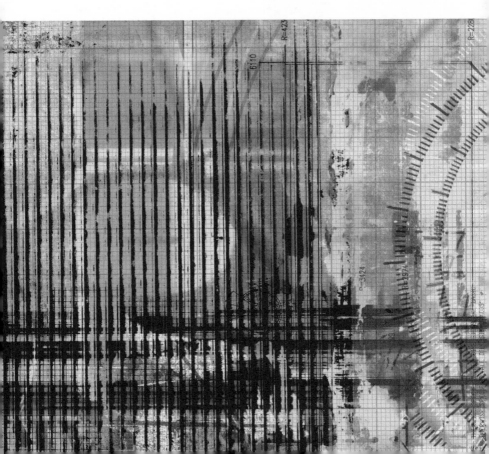

HOT STUFF

CAN WAR BE JUSTIFIED?

IT'S BETTER TO THINK BEFORE WAR THAN DURING IT.

"Hello, Javier," I said. "Come on in."

He entered and dropped into a chair. "How'd you know it was me? You didn't turn your head."

"You said, 'Knock, knock.' That's your signature greeting. What's up?"

"Professor T, do you think it's wrong for a Christian to go to war?"

I noticed his regulation haircut and remembered a previous conversation. "Does this have something to do with your being in the army reserves?"

"Yes." He paused. "See, I'm the first in my family to go to college, and I only joined the reserves for the educational benefits."

"Didn't you ever ask yourself what you thought about war?"

"Everybody said the Cold War was over. It never occurred to me that I might actually have to fight!"

"Now troops have been committed to Franistan, and if your reserve unit is called—"

"I'll be carrying a gun. And I want to be sure I'm doing the right thing."

I raised an eyebrow. "The next time you commit your life to an organization, Javier, wouldn't it be a good idea to decide whether you agree with its principles *first?*"

"Man, would it! But better late than never."

I smiled. "So what do you think so far?"

"God commanded wars in Old Testament times, right? And it stands to reason that sometimes a government has to use force to put down what's bad. But the Ten Commandments say, 'Thou shalt not kill.' And in the New Testament, Jesus said, 'All who draw the sword will die by the sword.'[1] I'm confused."

On my desk was a Bible. I pushed it over to him. "You quoted the traditional wording of the sixth commandment, but look at this modern translation."

"'You shall not *murder*,'" he read. "I don't get it. Aren't killing and murdering the same?"

"No. Murdering is deliberately taking innocent human life. It also includes taking guilty human life if the authority isn't yours because punishment is the responsibility of public officials, not vigilantes."

"What about Jesus saying that those who draw the sword will die by the sword? Shouldn't even public officials lay it down?"

"Some Christians think so. For much of the Christian era, though, most have believed Jesus meant something else—that we should never take the law into our own hands, never try to bring about the kingdom of God by worldly means, and never put our ultimate trust in violence. After all, Paul ought to have understood what Jesus meant, and *he* didn't condemn the use of force by public officials. He said that the ruler 'does not bear the sword for nothing. He is God's servant, an agent of wrath to bring punishment on the wrongdoer.'"[2]

"Then war and capital punishment are okay?"

"Let's say they *can* be okay. Rulers can also do wrong."

"So when are they right? Start with capital punishment."

"For capital punishment to be right, the guilty person would have to be convicted of a real crime in a fair trial, and the punishment would have to be fitting. Both the trial and the punishment would have to be carried out by public authority rather than private vigilantes. Even then it might be better to avoid capital punishment if there were another way to punish the criminal and keep him from doing further harm."

"Do *you* think there's another way?"

ASK ME ANYTHING   139

"A big debate about that is going on among Christians. I'd be glad to tell you my view, but—"

"Never mind, Prof," he interrupted. "Let's not open that can of worms today. Since I might have a gun in my hands soon, let's move on to war."

"Okay. For centuries Christian thinkers have been sharpening the criteria for distinguishing justified from unjustified wars."

"D'you mean criteria like, 'War may be waged only in self-defense'?"

"No, a criterion like that would make it wrong to come to the aid of your neighbor. I mean criteria like public authority, just cause, and right intention."

"What do those mean?"

"The first one means that only legitimate governments may wage war, not vigilantes or terrorists. The second one means that war may be waged only to save innocent life, to make sure people can live decently, or to protect their natural rights. The third one means your just cause has to be your *actual motive* for going to war."

"Is that last criterion like saying that it isn't enough to do the right thing—you have to do it for the right reason?"

"Exactly," I said. "The next three criteria are probability of success, comparative justice, and proportionality."

"I suppose probability of success means that even with good reasons, it's wrong to start a war you know you're going to lose."

"Right."

"But I can't guess the other two."

"Comparative justice means that the evils you're fighting against have to be bad enough to justify killing, and proportionality means you need good reason to believe the war will quench more evil than it causes."

"What kinds of evils, Professor T?"

"All kinds. Not just physical evils like bodily death or suffering, but spiritual evils too."

"You mean like becoming morally corrupt or losing faith in God?"

"Right. Finally, there is the criterion of last resort."

"I can figure that one out. You shouldn't go to war until you've tried everything else."

"No, until you've tried everything *reasonable*. There's always *something* else you might try, but it might be futile or even dangerous."

"Is that the last criterion? I have another question."

"Ask away."

"When you were explaining comparative justice, I noticed that you didn't say that the evils you're fighting against must be bad enough to justify murder—you said they must be bad enough to justify killing. Why?"

"That's because murder is always wrong, even in wartime. These criteria aren't in place to figure out when murder is okay, but to figure out when killing is murder and therefore wrong. Christians are not allowed to say, 'Let us do evil so that good may result.' That's the world's way of thinking. Our job is to do the right thing and let God take care of the results."

"I think I see that," Javier said slowly. "But here's what I don't get. If a particular war is justified, then in that case it's okay to kill the enemy, right? So how can an act of killing in wartime *ever* be murder?"

"Easy. For example, it's one thing to shoot soldiers, but it's another thing to blow up school buses. Do you understand?"

"Sure, I see that."

"The underlying principle is called discrimination. It says that directly intended attacks on noncombatants and nonmilitary targets are always wrong. Of course bombs don't always go where we want them to, but even accidental harm to noncombatants and nonmilitary targets should be minimized."

"Isn't this principle different from the others you mentioned, Professor Theophilus? The other seven were about when it's right to go to war, but this one is about how to fight when you do go to war."

"Right, and there are at least two more limits on how to fight. Two of the principles I mentioned earlier have a second role too."

"What do you mean?"

"Remember proportionality?"

"Of course."

"Applied to the question of *whether* to fight, it says you can't begin a war that would bring about more evil than it would stop. But applied to the question of *how* to fight, it says you can't use a *tactic* that would bring about more evil than it would stop."

"Oh, I see that. What's the other limit on how to fight?"

"Right intention. We talked about it earlier."

"Oh, yeah. It says the just cause must be your actual motive for going to war. It's like saying that you should only go to war to bring about a just peace. Right?"

"I couldn't have put it better. Now apply that principle to the question of *how* to fight."

"I guess you shouldn't use any tactic that would *prevent* a just peace."

"Exactly. So even though you're trying to win, you shouldn't commit any act or make any demand that would make it more difficult than it has to be for your enemies to reconcile with you someday."

"Man! My head is spinning. You don't make these decisions easy, do you?"

"They're *not* easy, but that's not my doing. War isn't the solution to sin, you know. Jesus Christ is the solution to sin. Fighting injustice is necessary, but it carries its own temptations to do wrong."

"I'll go think about Franistan," said Javier. He smiled wryly and offered me a little salute. I hesitated, smiled back, then made the sign of the cross.

HOMOPHOBIA, PART 1: RAGE

ALL THIS STUFF COMES FROM REAL CONVERSATIONS — NOT NECESSARILY THE SAME ONES.

"Are you Professor Theophilus?"

I turned. "That's me. Come in."

"My name's Lawrence. I'm telling you right out that I'm gay, and I came to complain about your talk yesterday about Constitutional liberties. It was bigoted and homophobic. I'm filing a formal protest to the people who run the Student Union speakers series."

At least he was direct. I waved him to a seat. "Help me out, Mr. Lawrence. How could—"

"Just Lawrence."

"Thank you. Now, how could my talk have been bigoted and homophobic when it didn't mention homosexuality?"

"I didn't actually hear the talk itself. I came in during Q&A."

"I see. And what did I say during Q&A?"

"You said gays have sex with animals."

I'm used to this sort of thing. "I'm afraid you weren't listening carefully."

"I remember distinctly," he declared. "A girl asked your opinion of laws against discrimination on the basis of sexual orientation, and you said gays have sex with animals."

"No," I replied, "what I said was that sexual orientation can mean many things. Some people are sexually oriented toward the opposite sex, others toward the same sex, others toward children, others toward animals, others toward cadavers. I said that I wondered where this trend will end."

"Then you admit that gays don't have sex with animals?"

"You brought that up," I reminded him. "I have no information on the point. I'm only suggesting that not all orientations are morally equivalent." He said nothing but showed no inclination to leave. "Do *you* think all orientations are morally equivalent?" I queried.

"I won't even dignify that question with an answer," he said. "But I know what you think of *my* orientation. I'm sick of you phony Christians with your filthy hypocrisy about the love of God."

"So you know I'm a Christian."

"Who doesn't? The holy, the sanctimonious, the Most Excellent Professor Theophilus of Post-Everything State University — what else would he be? The whole school reeks of you, of you and the other so-called Christian so-called professors. That's why I walked in on your Q&A. I wanted to see you spit venom."

"My goodness. Have I said anything venomous?"

"It's what you're thinking that's venomous."

"I see," I said, smiling. "Why don't you stop being bashful and tell me what's bothering you?"

"You must think you're funny."

"I'm serious. Tell your complaints one by one, and I'll answer them."

"You wouldn't answer. I have too many."

"Try me. I'll give short answers."

He cocked his head and peered at me. "You mean it, don't you?"

"I wouldn't say it if I didn't."

"One at a time?"

"One at a time."

"All right, here's the first: Christians are hypocrites. You're always running down gays, but what about the other things your Bible condemns, like divorce and remarriage? It's other people's sins that bother you, not your own."

I laughed. "If you'd spent any time around me, you'd know that I'm just as hard on the sins of heterosexuals as on those of homosexuals.

Easy divorce is a prime example of how one bad thing leads to another—in our case the loss of the ability to make any distinctions about sexual acts at all."

Ignoring the reply, he went on to his next complaint. "You're intolerant. You reject people like me just because we're different from you."

"Me reject you?" I said. "Aren't you the one who rejects what is different from yourself? Don't you reject the challenge of the other sex?"

"I don't need the other sex. I have a committed relationship with my partner."

"Research shows that homosexuals with partners don't stop cruising; they just cruise less.[1] When they don't think straights are listening, gay writers say the same."[2]

"So what if it's true? There's nothing wrong with gay love anyway."

"Tell me what's loving about sex acts that cause bleeding, choking, disease, and pain," I suggested quietly. "You might start by explaining the meaning of the medical term Gay Bowel Syndrome[3] or how people get herpes lesions on their tonsils."

"You're—how can you even say that?" he demanded. "How dare you tell me who to love?"

"I don't think I am telling you who to love."

"Oh, no? Then what are you telling me?"

"That there is nothing loving about mutual self-destruction."

"You must think my relationship with my partner is just dirt!"

"No, I respect friendship wherever I find it—your friendship with your partner included. It's just that sex doesn't make every kind of friendship better."

"Why not? Are you anti-sex or something?"

"Not at all," I said, "but would you say that sex improves the friendship of a father with his daughter?" Seeing from his face that he didn't, I continued. "You get my point. Nor does sex improve the friendship of two men."

"That's where you're wrong. Gay sex is just as natural for some people as straight sex is for other people."

"What's *natural*," I said, "is what corresponds to our design—what unlocks our inbuilt potential instead of thwarting it. One of the purposes of marital sex is to get us outside of Self and its concerns to achieve intimacy with someone who is Really Other." *Was he listening?* "I'm sorry, Lawrence—I really am—but having sex with another man can't do that. It's too much like loving your own reflection."

I was about to go on, but he abruptly changed the subject: "It's attitudes like yours that killed Matthew Shepard."

"Surely you don't imagine that the thugs who killed Matthew Shepard were *Christians*, do you?" I smiled, but seeing that he misunderstood my intention I made my face serious and tried again. "Lawrence, I deplore the violence that killed Matthew Shepard, and I'm glad those men were caught. But shouldn't we also grieve the urge that caused Matthew Shepard to be sexually attracted to violent strangers?"

He said only, "You hate me."

I paused to study him. Did he really believe that, or was it a smokescreen? "I don't hate you," I said. "I love you." I paused. "I'd like to be with you forever in heaven."

Lawrence's face displayed shock, as though he had been hit in the stomach. Then he looked confused. The expression of confusion was instantaneously replaced by an expression of anger. For one split second, it had looked as if the shutters were open. *God in heaven,* I thought, *I need help.* How could they be pried back up? "*My* love isn't really the issue for you, is it?" I asked.

"What do you mean?"

"It's God's. God's love is the issue for you."

For a few seconds there was no reaction. Then it came. "You're *@!$*#! right God's love is the issue for me," he said. "*Your* God's love. The lying God who says He loves man but who hates me for loving men."

"Do you think God hates you?"

"Doesn't He?"

"Why do you think so?"

"Doesn't your Bible say that? It calls people like me abomination."

"It calls what you *do* abomination. There's a difference."

"There's no difference. I do what I am."

I considered. "Could it be," I said, "that you want God to love you *less?*"

"Less!" he spat.

"Yes. Don't you know what love is?"

"Acceptance."

"Acceptance of what kills you? Consider another view: Love is a commitment of the will to the true good of the other person."

"What?"

"I said love is a commitment of the will to the true good of the other person."

"I don't get what you're saying."

"Sure you do. The lover wants what's good for the beloved."

He hesitated. "I suppose."

"Good. Now think. If that's what love is, then a *perfect* Lover would want the *perfect* good of the beloved. And do you see what that means? He would loathe and detest whatever destroyed the beloved's good— no matter how much the beloved desired it."

I couldn't read the look on his face, so I plowed on. "That's what sin does—it destroys us. Yours destroys you; mine destroys me. And so the Lover doesn't accept it; He hates it with an inexorable hatred. To cut the cancer out of us, He will do whatever it takes—like a surgeon. No, more than like a surgeon. If you let Him, He will even take the cancer upon Himself and die in your place."

Still inscrutable, he kept his eyes in front of him, just avoiding my own.

I asked, "What happens, then, if you refuse to let go of what destroys you? What happens if you say to the divine and perfect Lover who wants your complete and perfect good, 'I bind myself to my destruction! Accept me—and my destruction with me! I refuse to enter heaven except in the company of death!'"

Neither of us spoke.

Lawrence rose from his chair and walked out the door.

HOMOPHOBIA, PART 2: THE SEEKER

LAWRENCE WOULD HAVE TOLD ME THAT GUYS LIKE ADAM DON'T EXIST.

"It wasn't easy finding your office," said my visitor as he took a seat. "This building is like a rabbit warren."

"Yes," I said, "for my first couple of years, I had to leave a trail of crumbs each day to find my way back out. Have we met?"

"No, I'm in Antediluvian Studies—a grad student. Adam Apollolas."

"M. E. Theophilus." We shook hands.

"You *are* the same Theophilus who wrote the 'Homophobia' dialogue for *Nounless* webzine, aren't you? I was hoping to talk with you about it."

"Busted," I smiled. "What would you like to know about it?"

"Was it based on a real conversation?"

"Yes and no; it was a composite. A homosexual student really did visit to accuse me of saying that gays have sex with animals. The rest is from real life, too, but not necessarily from the same conversation."

"But it can't possibly be true that all of the homosexuals who speak with you are as angry and closed-minded as he was."

"No, of course not."

"Then why did you portray him that way in the dialogue?"

"Would you have me pretend that *nobody* in the homosexual life is angry and closed-minded? A good many are like that—you should see my letters—and I try to show my readers the dynamics of more than one kind of conversation. You see, when people have honest questions, you try to answer them, but when they only churn out smokescreens, then you blow the smoke away."

"So you'd be open to different kinds of conversation."

"Of course," I said. I smiled and added, "Are we, perhaps, having one right now?"

His eyebrows lifted. "Am I that obvious?"

"It was just a shot in the dark. So what did you really want to talk about?"

"I'm not very ideological, but I guess you could call me a Seeker. See, I've been in the gay life for five years, but lately I've been having second thoughts. I'm not asking you to convert me, understand? I thought I'd just hear what you have to say and then go away and think about it."

"What have you been having second thoughts about?"

He hesitated. "Are you going to use this conversation in one of your dialogues?"

"If I did, I'd make sure you couldn't be identified. You can speak freely."

"Well—" He hesitated. "One thing is intimacy. I've never had problems finding sex, but it's more or less anonymous. That didn't bother me at first, but now it's getting me down."

"Is it always anonymous?"

"No, the first time I had gay sex was in a steady relationship. I've been in two or three others too—for a month, two months, a year. But they were never what you'd call faithful, you know what I mean? It's as though there had to be other sexual outlets for the relationship to work at all. I'm starting to want . . . I don't know. Something more."

"I follow you."

He paused. "Another thing. I want to be a dad. That doesn't fit the stereotype, does it? Are you surprised to hear me say it?"

"Not at all."

"Then you're the only one. My friends don't get it. One said, 'Why not just get a turkey baster and make an arrangement with a lesbian?' But that's not what I want. I used to say to myself, 'Get used to it. You

can't have everything you want.' But that doesn't work for me anymore."
After a second he spoke again. "There's one more thing."

"What's that?"

"God."

"God? How so?"

"Oh, I go to church sometimes. Now *that* must surprise you."

"No. What kind of church?"

"Different kinds. I didn't go to any church at first. My family never went to church. Most of my gay friends don't have any use for God. Then I started going to a gay church and that was okay for a while. But I think I might want the real stuff, do you know what I mean? Or else nothing."

"I think so. You don't have any doubts about what the real stuff is?"

"No. I'm not saying I believe in Jesus, but—" He thought for a moment. "The gay church said you can be a Christian and still live a gay life. I don't think I ever really believed that. I read a book that the minister in the gay church recommended."

"Yes?"

"The title was something like *Sex and Dirt.* I'm leaving something out. Hold on, it'll come to me."

"I know the book."

"Oh, good. Then you probably remember how the author says that when the Bible lays down sexual rules, they're just purity codes—not moral laws—so you don't have to keep them."

"Sure."

"He had me going for a while—right up to where he said, 'That's why even having sex with animals is okay,' or words to that effect. Just what the guy in your dialogue accused *you* of saying gay people think. I could see that the author's conclusion followed from his premises—but after that, I didn't have any use for his premises, if you see what I mean."

"I see exactly what you mean. So where does all this leave you?"

"Like I said, I want to hear you out, and then I'll go away and think about it."

"That's fine, Adam, but just what is it that you want to hear me out about?"

"I think what I'm missing is the Big Picture about sex. If there is a Big Picture about sex."

"There is indeed a Big Picture about sex."

"Draw it, then. Paint it. Lecture me, even. That is," he added, "if you don't mind."

I had to laugh. "You asked me before if I was going to use this conversation in one of my dialogues. If I do, nobody will believe it. They'll call it contrived."

"Why?"

"Because you've set the stage too well. Your 'second thoughts' anticipate everything I'd like to say. And now you ask for a lecture!"

"After seven years of higher education, I'm used to lectures. You do your professor thing, and I'll listen. If I want to argue—believe me, I know how—I'll come back another day."

I collected my thoughts. "All right, Adam. The main point of Christian sexual morality is that human nature is *designed*. We need to live a certain way because we're designed to live that way."

He said, "I can see design in an organ like the heart. Human nature—that's a little too big for me."

"Then let's start with the heart. Do you see how every part works together toward its purpose, its function?"

"Sure. You've got nerves and valves and pumping chambers, all for moving blood."

"Right. If you think about the sexual powers instead of the heart, it's just the same. The key to understanding a design is to recognize its purposes. For the heart, the purpose is pumping blood; for the sexual powers—you tell me."

"Pleasure?"

"Think about it. Would you say pleasure is the purpose of eating?"

"No, I'd say nourishment is the purpose of eating, and pleasure is just the result."

"If you thought pleasure was the purpose of eating, what would you do if I offered you pleasant-tasting poison?"

"Eat it."

"And what would happen?"

"I'd get sick."

"But if you understood that nourishment is the purpose of eating and pleasure merely the result, *then* what would you do if I offered you pleasant-tasting poison?"

"Refuse it and ask for food instead."

"It's the same with the sexual powers. Pleasure is a result of their use, but it's not the purpose of their use. The purposes can tell you which kinds of sexual activity are good and which aren't; by itself, pleasure can't."

"So what are the purposes of the sexual powers?"

"You've told me already; you just didn't realize you were doing so."

"I have? When?"

"When you were telling me your doubts about the homosexual life. There were three of them. The third was religious. For now let's just talk about the first and second. What was the first again?"

"Intimacy. Bonding."

"And the second?"

"Having children."

"Then you won't be surprised to hear that one inbuilt purpose of the sexual powers is to bond a man with a woman and the other is to have and raise children."

"If bonding is good, why not use the sexual powers to bond a man with a man?"

"Has that worked in your case, Adam?"

"Well, no. That's what I was complaining about."

"You see, that's no accident. Bonding man with man is contrary to the design."

"You *say* that, but how do you *know*?"

"There are two reasons. First, man and woman are complementary. They're not just *different*, but they *match* as well. There is something in male emotional design to which only the female can give completion and something in female emotional design to which only the male can give completion. When same mates with same, that can't happen. Instead of balancing each other, they unbalance each other."

"What's the other reason?"

"The other reason is that the linkage of same with same is sterile. You've complained about that too."

"But sometimes a man can't produce children with a woman either."

"The mating of same with same isn't *accidentally* sterile, Adam, as the union of a particular man with a particular woman might be; it's *inherently* sterile. A husband and wife who are unable to have a baby haven't set themselves against their own inbuilt purposes. A man and man who have sex together have."

He grinned. "There's always the turkey baster."

"But when your friend made that suggestion, you refused, didn't you? What was your reason?"

"I'm not sure. I just think a kid needs a mom and a dad."

"That's exactly right. Male and female complement and complete each other not just in having children but also in rearing them. Women are better designed for nurture; men are better designed for protection. Besides, two dads can't model male-female relationships. Neither can two moms."

Adam was silent as he digested this. "You know," he said finally, "this isn't at all what I expected you to talk about."

"What did you expect me to talk about?"

"Disease." He paused. "Now that I think about it, you didn't say much about disease in that dialogue I read either."

"I should think you already know the deadliness of your way of life."

"I suppose so. But it does seem unfair. Why should gay sex be less healthy than any other kind?"

"Don't we come right back to the design? Start with the fact that not all orifices are created equal."

"Hmm."

"Hmm?"

"I think I'll go do what I said I'd do: go away and think about it all. In the meantime, Professor, I think you have a problem."

"Do I?"

"That is, if you do intend to use this chat of ours in one of your dialogues."

"And what might this problem be?"

"We've talked too long. Your dialogues are always shorter than this. This one is way over."

I smiled. "I'll talk to my editor about it."

HOT LETTERS

TARGETING NONCOMBATANTS

Dear Professor Theophilus:

I was recently discussing your dialogue,"Can War Be Justified?" with my seventeen-year-old son. In the context of the 9/11 tragedy, we were talking about terrorism and the evil of aiming at nonmilitary targets.

He raised the matter of the bombing of Nagasaki and Hiroshima during World War II, pointing to the obvious fact that this action purposely took the lives of many civilians, apparently violating the principle of discrimination. I was unable to mount a good response. Have you any thoughts to help me take the discussion further?

Reply: Your son raises an excellent question, and I think he's right. The bombings of Hiroshima and Nagasaki violated the discrimination principle because they deliberately targeted noncombatants. Some people seek to justify them on grounds of the proportionality principle, holding that if we had not bombed Hiroshima and Nagasaki, then the war would have been so prolonged that ultimately even more people would have died. Even if this claim were true, the flaw in the reasoning is that it pits the proportionality principle against the discrimination principle—as though what we consider a good result could justify evil means. That is exactly how the perpetrators of the 9/11 atrocity reasoned, and such thinking is plainly condemned by the apostle Paul in Romans 3:8. We have to satisfy both the discrimination *and* the proportionality principle; it won't do to say that if we satisfy the latter well enough, then the former can be set aside.

Behind the principles of just war is the God-given idea that it is categorically wrong to deliberately take innocent human life. The principles are not intended to tell us when murder is okay; murder is never okay. Rather, their purpose is to tell us whether war can be waged *without* murder, and if so how.

May the Father bless your fatherhood and may He continue to illuminate your conversations with your son.

Grace and peace,
Professor Theophilus

I HAVE ONE TRUE ENEMY

Dear Professor Theophilus:

I have only one true enemy. He's my dad. He and I have never been close, but when I was in high school we grew even further apart. I remember all the times my father beat up my siblings and me. He always told us—and still tells us, sometimes hitting us while telling us—how stupid we are. Now that I'm in college, he still does these things, but I'm usually not there. It's very hard for me to believe that God really cares about us when He lets everyone suffer. I don't know, maybe He just made us, got bored, and left us to do our own thing.

I don't understand my father. He acts as if the way he treats us is perfectly fine and as though we ask for it. I hope I never become like him, although I can sometimes see (and feel) myself as his mirror image, and I hate him. That is another reason why it's so hard for me to be a Christian. How can I forgive someone who is so self-righteous (and always, ALWAYS right) when he continues to destroy me and my family?

Reply: You ask two questions: How can you forgive your father for making his family suffer? And how can you believe in God's love when God allows such suffering to continue?

We can't do without fathering. Our earthly fathers were intended, through their love, to give us glimpses of the love of our Father in heaven. It is exactly because this is what they were intended to be that we suffer so greatly when they fall short. When they do fall short — when, like your father, they fail to be likenesses of the heavenly Father and instead become fountains of pain — that doesn't mean that we can do without fathering. What it means is that we must hold out our arms and get our fathering directly from God. If we refuse to do this because of our resentment of our earthly fathers, then we merely become like those earthly fathers, continuing the deadly cycle. You've caught a glimpse of that already.

That's why I think that a choice between two paths lies before you. One path is to resent your earthly father so much that you become like him, drowning in hatred and rejecting your Father in heaven too. The other is to depend on your heavenly Father so faithfully that you become like *Him* instead, overflowing with the strength that is sufficient even to forgive your earthly father.

Here is the bad news: If you try to do this by sheer willpower, you'll fail. It can be done only in the power of God. Therefore, trust Him. Do not ask for proof of His love before you trust; only trust, and then you will receive the proof. If you wonder how you can believe in His love even though He permits us to make each other suffer, remember that in His love He took the worst of our suffering upon Himself. I realize that I repeat this often in this column; it is such a great mystery that even the angels long to look into it (see 1 Peter 1:12).

Have I answered both questions?

A final word: If your father is still physically injuring the younger members of your family, he must be made to stop. Report him to the authorities. This is not a violation of the commandment to honor parents because it is not a part of honor to allow him to do injury to others.

Grace and peace,
Professor Theophilus

CAN'T ANYONE TELL ME WHY?

Dear Professor Theophilus:

I don't know if this is the right place to send a letter like this, but I'm at my wit's end! I've asked pastors, friends, parents, God, and message boards this question and still haven't gotten an intelligent answer that I can live with. Why are homosexual acts wrong? I am a Christian and believe very much in the Bible, but this part of it always stumps me.

The reasons why other sins are wrong are obvious. Murder, rape, adultery, theft—they all harm other people. But homosexual acts don't harm anyone. People say it's not natural, but it occurs in nature among animals. People say gays can't procreate, but since when is sex even mostly about procreation? It's about love, intimacy, and pleasure, and gays can experience all of that. Also, what about people who are born sexually ambiguous? Who are they supposed to fall in love with? If you are born with the physical traits of both a male and a female, are you gay no matter whom you sleep with or are you straight no matter whom you sleep with? It just doesn't add up to me.

I don't believe in disregarding parts of the Bible that I don't agree with, so it's important to me that I settle this in my mind. If you can't help me, point me to someone who can! Thank you.

Reply: Don't blame the other people you've talked to for being unable to answer your questions. If we lived in normal times, it would be better not to discuss certain sins at all. Because we live in abnormal times, we have to. But it makes people uncomfortable to discuss them, so they never learn how to give good answers. Actually I've dealt with this topic pretty often; you can find what I've written about it before at www.boundless.org. In the meantime, I'd like you to reconsider your assumptions. I suspect that you've been listening to propaganda because you're making some serious mistakes. Once those are cleared up, I think the answer to your question will jump out at you.

The meaning of the natural. Our nature is how God designed us, so what's natural for human beings isn't whatever you can find some animal doing; it's whatever fulfills our design. Men and women were plainly designed for each other—not men for men, nor women for women.

What harms whom. The idea that homosexual acts don't harm anybody isn't even close to being true; they harm those who commit them at every level—physical, emotional, and spiritual. To begin with the most obvious—the physical—how could it *not* harm a man to suffer rectal trauma because a large object has been repeatedly forced into an opening that was designed for a radically different function? Lesbian sex is no picnic either; the rate of syphilis among women who practice homosexual acts is nineteen times higher than the rate among women who don't.

Other levels of harm. At the emotional and spiritual levels, the damage of homosexual acts is less obvious but just as grave. Consider emotional harm. God designed the male-female pair to balance each other; by contrast, same-same mating drives the partners to extremes. Instead of balancing each other, they reinforce each other. If you want an example, think of the anonymous, no-brakes promiscuity of men who have sex with hundreds, even thousands, of other men. Now consider spiritual harm. In homosexual acts you're seeking union with someone who is only your own mirror image, so in a way, you're still trapped inside yourself. You haven't experienced the power of marital sex to take you *beyond* the Self; you're rejecting the challenge of union with someone who is really Other. In that way, homosexual acts are less like marital love and more like masturbation with another body.

So-called ambiguous gender. Genetically, every child is either male or female. To say that a girl whose sexual organs resemble a boy's is part-boy is like saying that a baby whose arms resemble flippers is part-seal. She doesn't need to mate with other girls any more than he needs to eat raw fish. What she needs is restorative surgery, which usually corrects the problem.

How pleasure is related to sex. No, pleasure is not the purpose of sex. Of course sex *is* pleasurable (God made it that way), and it's right for a husband and wife to enjoy that pleasure (God intended that). But to say that pleasure is the *purpose* of sex—to say that it's *why* God invented sex—to say that it's what tells us *when sex is right and when it's not*—is quite another matter. You see, you can get pleasure from misusing God's gifts as well as from using them properly. If pleasure were the purpose of eating, then whatever caused eating-pleasure would be good; we should do as some Romans were said to do at banquets, vomiting in order to eat some more. If pleasure were the purpose of sex, then whatever caused sex-pleasure would be good. Some people get sex-pleasure from kids, from corpses, or from physical pain and humiliation. Pleasure wouldn't justify those perversions, would it? Then why would it justify sodomy?

The first purpose of sex. The first purpose of sex is procreation—having children. To say that sex isn't about having babies is like saying that eating isn't about taking in nutrition. Besides, if sex isn't about having babies, how do you suppose that God *did* intend us to procreate? I'm not just talking about the fact that homosexual acts are sterile, although that's part of the problem. The procreative purpose of sex applies not only to bearing children but also to raising them. A child needs a mom and a dad—one of each.

The second purpose of sex. The second purpose of sex is intimacy. You're right about that point, but only partly right. What you mean by intimacy is feeling close, and feelings aren't enough. An episode of the Jerry Springer Show featured a guest who claimed to have "married" her horse. I suppose she "felt close" to it, but when we say that the second purpose of sex is intimacy, that's not what we mean. Marital intimacy is the unique bond of self-giving brought about by the complementary union of husband and wife in a procreative partnership. They are complementary because each sex provides something missing from the makeup of the other. Two men do not complement each other, and neither do two women. They can have warm friendships, but sex doesn't improve these friendships; it only degrades them.

For Christians, sex has a third purpose too. The Christian marital union was intended by God to be a sign of Christ's union with the Church. You can read about this in Ephesians 5.

Have I answered your question?

Grace and peace,
Professor Theophilus

HOMOPHOBIA: THE FALLOUT

"Homophobia: An Unfinished Story" sparked more e-mail than any other dialogues I've written. Some readers accused me of lacking love:

If I wrote down one of my dreams, would you publish me? After all, it would be a *#*! of a lot more believable than this #*!@. Why do you assume that your readers are unbelievably dumb? Is it because they ARE dumb (college students, no less), or is it because you like to deceive yourself into thinking that? One of the saddest gay-bashing attempts I've come across.

Others, like this one, thanked me for having love:

I really enjoyed your article about homophobia. As the Christian daughter of a gay man, this issue is very dear to my heart. I see how destructive homosexuality is to my father and others every day. I am so glad to see your words stressing God's love as His purpose for wanting us not to sin. It's a relief that you speak the truth without bigotry.

Some asked heart-wrenching questions, like this one:

My brother is gay, and your column has helped me to focus my approach to him. However, he recently informed me that he has joined a new church whose founder has had an entirely NEW New Testament "channeled" through her by Christ! He says

that the NEW New Testament is much more "tolerant" of different lifestyles and strives
toward unity of all religious beliefs. How do I approach this?

I responded:

> We all cook up rationalizations and excuses when we
> do wrong, and your brother's is just a little weirder
> than most. You should keep praying, keep loving him,
> try not to panic, and avoid confusing love with
> approval. If your brother is at all open to reason, point
> out that an all-knowing God would not have to revise
> His perfect Bible and that a "unity" among religions
> that hold diametrically opposite views would be
> impossible. Most important is to explain that no lov-
> ing Father would "tolerate" anything that destroys His
> children. God loves your brother too much to keep
> silent about his self-destructive desires.

Here's another letter that pulled at my heart:

I just found out that my boyfriend is gay. I love him very much, and he loves me
the best way he can. He hates these feelings he has for men. He wants to change and
has been praying for these thoughts and desires to be taken away. My family is pray-
ing for him too. Is there anything else I should do for him? He is a Christian, but I
believe part of his problem is that his father suffered from a mental disorder, so he never
really had a chance to love him. Now he's reaching out for male love in another way.

I responded:

> The good news for your boyfriend is that change is
> possible for those who really want to change.
> Thousands have come out of homosexuality, and
> the Bible too confirms the possibility of change (see
> 1 Corinthians 6:9-11). I don't mean that change is

easy, but nothing can limit the power of God. Have your boyfriend contact Exodus Global Alliance, an umbrella organization of Christian ministries that offers support to men and women seeking to overcome homosexuality, at www.exodusglobalalliance.org. If he's Catholic, then have him contact Courage Apostolate at http://www.couragerc.net. In the meantime, do something for yourself: Get in touch with Parents and Friends of Ex-Gays & Gays, an Exodus-affiliated network of parents, friends, and families whose loved ones struggle with homosexuality. The web address is www.pfox.org.

With the following correspondent, I continued for two rounds. Although she offered as true certain claims I've challenged in other writings—for example, the prevalence of the so-called committed gay relationship—I don't think love would have been served by arguing with her about them. There is a time and place for everything, and the real issues between us were quite different.

"Homophobia: Rage" is a thinly-veiled attempt to provide thoughtless, spoon-fed dialogue to college students who may encounter gay students on their campuses. It seems to be a way to prevent young college students from actually listening to the person who is merely trying to defend themselves—how they feel and who they love.

The author's arguments were almost painful to read. I don't know why he feels the need to defend his beliefs. Simply put, he believes homosexuality is wrong. End of story. No one can really argue with that since he has a right to his opinion. Don't I wish this were the scenario. Instead, he spreads misinformation. The truth of the matter is that both heterosexuals and homosexuals contract sexually transmitted diseases, are promiscuous, and have sexual relations that include nonprocreative sexual activities.

How do you expect homosexuals to react to these arguments? With smiles? He's essentially calling all gay people immoral heathens instead of recognizing that there is great *diversity among people in the gay community. By pretending to be reasonable, the author tries to craft a tone and attitude that would push the buttons of anyone who was gay or a friend of gays—not because he's right but because he's so obtuse and self-righteous. If anything, this is what pushes many homosexuals to allegedly hate Christians.*

What is my solution? Leave each other alone. Gay people calling themselves a "couple" or "married" DOES NOT affect you in any way. Go preach to your fellow believers but leave us alone.

Here's how I replied:

Thank you for your letter. I'm sad that you're upset. It surprises me a bit that you think the remarks of my fictional character Lawrence are unrealistic and stereotypical. His opening accusation comes from a real-life conversation with one of my homosexual students. The rest of the things he says seem rather like the remarks in your own letter.

For example, don't you express the same hot, defensive anger toward me that Lawrence expressed? Like Lawrence, don't you put words in my mouth (like "immoral heathens") instead of responding to the words I actually used? Most important, don't you hold the same opinion that Lawrence does about what it means for me to love you? You see, when I come across someone who is destroying her life, I think love means that I should care enough to urge her to live. You think love means that I should walk on by. Thank God for the people who tried to talk to me when I was killing myself.

I'm sad, too, that you think my picture of the homosexual life is distorted. My friends who have left the gay and lesbian life seem to think it's pretty accurate. If you ever have second thoughts about the life—perhaps you have had some already—please remember that change is possible. Christ changed my friends, He changed me when I was experiencing a different kind of brokenness (though just as deep), and He would love to show you what He has in mind for you.

If you're determined to hear hatred when I speak of hope, I don't know what else to say. But I hope that won't be the case. Lawrence's story isn't finished yet. Neither is yours. May the grace of God be with you.

Finally, a young homosexual woman not only wrote several letters about "Homophobia: Rage" but also composed a paragraph-by-paragraph commentary. Her correspondence came to more than three thousand words, so I've strung together only the highlights. For context, I've also patched in two of my own comments from "Homophobia: Rage."

I have SERIOUS issues with how you characterized your opponent. He is illogical, stereotypical, and unforgivably DUMB. If an actual gay student talked to you that way, I think he must be pretty dumb too. I would like to see how you respond to my points about disease and difference in same-gender relationships.

[You said], "Tell me what's loving about sex acts that cause bleeding, choking, disease, and pain." These very same sex acts can be engaged in by mixed-gender couples. A dominatrix can make a man bleed with whips or razors. A man's penis can choke a woman.

[You said], "Aren't you the one who rejects what is different than yourself? Don't you reject the challenge of the other sex?" I was born and raised in [America]. My girlfriend spent the first thirteen years of her life [overseas]. That in itself is a difference. We have very different personalities—I'm vocal and emotional; she's quiet and analytical. We look very different—I weigh, literally, almost twice as much as she does. We are of different religions—I'm a Vodoun/Witchcraft syncretist; she's a Gnostic Christian.

I replied:

> Thank you for your note. Concerning the dialogue, yes, it's just as you seem to suspect: Everything that my fictional character Lawrence said is taken either from conversations with, letters from, or articles by people leading the homosexual life. Perhaps that will absolve me of stereotyping or disrespect. Concerning difference, I think you misunderstood my point. The sexual difference is unlike other kinds of difference because men and women are designed for each other; each lacks something that only the other can provide. Finally, concerning disease, you're quite right that if a man and woman engage in sexual practices for which their bodies are not designed, they will suffer the same ill effects that homosexuals suffer for engaging in them. Please, my dear, consider the implications.
>
> In the love of Christ,
> Professor Theophilus

ONE LAST LETTER

Dear Professor Theophilus:

I am not a Christian, but I am writing to tell you that you are right and I was wrong.

I am twenty years old, and since age thirteen I have been "lesbian-identified." What this means is that while I was never actually involved with a woman, I was fluent in the language of gay culture: I had gay friends, attended gay pride parades in San Francisco, and had a hidden but extensive library containing everything from the "classic" gay novels to lesbian "erotica" (read: pornography).

In the summer of 1999, two very important things happened. The first was that I lost my virginity to a man with the support and encouragement of my Christian mother, who thought it would "cure" me. (I kept my hands over my face the entire time, and I didn't feel particularly healthy afterward.) The second was that I became seriously ill. It turns out that these two events were not connected, though at first I feared they might be.

Afterward, I was bedridden for a year, and during that time I discovered your writing in Boundless. An emotional battle began that has lasted almost two years, and I am finally throwing in the towel. Why? Let me share with you three random events from my life:

1. I received a phone call from my friend X. (She used to have a recognizably female name, Z, but she had it legally changed because she wanted something that was gender nonspecific. I'm not kidding.) She called to tell me that her girlfriend had decided to have her breasts surgically removed.
2. I visited the website of a lesbian magazine and found an article on how to use needles as an aid to sexual pleasure. The author recommended having benzalkonium chloride towelettes on hand to wipe up the blood.
3. A straight female friend e-mailed me from college asking for advice. Here is an excerpt:

> I have suddenly become sexually brazen, and it scares me a little. . . . I think that it's about time, though, that I start enjoying myself and stop giving myself guilt/head trips about it in the process. But what really irks me is that the people I meet are either in the army or navy, players, spending just the weekend, on a road trip, or leaving the state in a matter of weeks. . . . I can't help but feel that some or a lot of this is a little empty.

When women want to cut off their female organs, when hurting each other with needles is considered a turn-on, and when promiscuous girls feel guilty about feeling guilty (as though they just aren't liberated enough), something has gone terribly, terribly awry. I have been a faithful reader of yours—I even own one of your books,

Written on the Heart—and I've been hopping mad at you more times than I can count. The funny thing is, I keep coming back to your writing. I think it has to do with "what you can't not know." And I've always respected the fact that you would rather offend your readers than coddle them or compromise your message. The truth is surprisingly effective. Keep telling it, and I'll keep listening. I may even end up a Christian someday.

Reply: Thank you for writing. You don't have a question for me, but I couldn't let your letter go unanswered.

According to my faith, God cares more about a single soul than the rest of the universe—and it means more than the rest of the universe to me if, by His grace, my writing makes a difference to a single soul. I'm glad you're one of the souls to which it has made a difference. Though I understand that you aren't a Christian, I hope you won't be offended if I pray for you. My prayer is that some day soon, you, too, will be willing to meet this God of amazing mercies who has healing in His wings.

Grace and peace,
Professor Theophilus

NOTES

CHAPTER 2

1. 1 Corinthians 10:23; compare 1 Corinthians 6:12. See also proverbs about wisdom.
2. See Matthew 19:10-12.
3. See 1 Corinthians 7.

CHAPTER 8

1. The Joint Declaration on the Doctrine of Justification can be found at www. vatican.va/roman_curia/pontifical_councils/chrstuni/documents/rc_pc_chrstuni_ doc_31101999_cath-luth-joint-declaration_en.html. If this URL is changed, go instead to the list of documents at www.vatican.va/roman_curia/pontifical_ councils/chrstuni/sub-index/index_lutheran-fed.htm, scroll down, and click on the link named "Common declaration on the Doctrine of Justification issued by the Catholic Church and the Lutheran World Federation [31 October 1999]."

CHAPTER 9

1. G. K. Chesterton, *Collected Works, Volume XVI: The Autobiography* (San Francisco: Ignatius Press, 1988), p. 212.
2. For details, see www.boundless.org/2000/regulars/office_hours/a0000160.html.

CHAPTER 10

1. Romans 1:20, emphasis added.

CHAPTER 11

1. Roger Williams, *The Bloudy Tenent of Persecution for Cause of Conscience* (London, 1644).

CHAPTER 13

1. The Eclipsitarians are imaginary, but they closely resemble several real-world denominations. In a press conference immediately after the August 5, 2003 vote of the Episcopal House of Bishops to elevate Canon Gene Robinson to the office

of Bishop of New Hampshire, Robinson remarked, "Just simply to say that it goes against tradition and the teaching of the church and scripture does not necessarily make it wrong." Gene Robinson, quoted in "Episcopal Church Confirms Gay Bishop," *The Washington Post*, August 6, 2003. The House of Bishops had previously authorized local dioceses to draw up rites for the blessing of same-sex unions.

CHAPTER 14

1. C. S. Lewis, *The Abolition of Man* (New York: Macmillan, 1955), pp. 54-56.
2. *Westminster Larger Catechism*, http://www.ccel.org/creeds/westminster-larger-cat.html

CHAPTER 15

1. Matthew 26:52.
2. Romans 13:4.

CHAPTER 16

1. Summarizing the findings of Alan R. Bell and Martin S. Weinberg, Louis Berman reports that "gays who are 'close-coupled' . . . don't abandon cruising; they do less cruising." Louis Berman, "Long-Term Gay Relationships," NARTH 1996 Collected Papers, National Association for Research and Therapy of Homosexuality.
2. Gay activist Andrew Sullivan in his book *Virtually Normal* (New York: Knopf, 1995) tries to have it both ways. On the one hand, he argues that the extreme instability of homosexual relationships is due to social disapproval; if only homosexuals could "marry," they would become more faithful to each other. But in his final chapter, he lets the cat out of the bag. It turns out that he doesn't expect gay "marriage" to change homosexual behavior so much as to change *heterosexual* behavior. According to Sullivan, social approval of homosexual liaisons would be good for straight culture because it would teach straights to accept infidelity. As he puts it, there is "more likely to be a greater understanding of the need for extramarital outlets between two men than between a man and a woman" (p. 202). In another book, *Love Undetectable* (New York: Knopf, 1998), he releases an even bigger cat from the bag. As he explains in a letter to *Salon* magazine, the book defends "the beauty and mystery and spirituality of sex, *including anonymous sex*" (emphasis added). The letter was published in the magazine on December 15, 1999, and is available at ww2.salon.com/letters/1999/12/15/sullivan index.html.

3. The term *Gay Bowel Syndrome* was first used in *Annals of Clinical Laboratory Science* 6 (1976): 184 to describe a group of bowel diseases such as amebiasis, giardiasis, shigellosis, and hepatitis A that are rare in the general population but common among male homosexuals in the United States. *The New England Journal of Medicine* 302 (1980): 435-438 stated that "among male homosexuals, these diseases are rampant because of oral-anal practices involving the ingestion of fecal matter." Other sources suggest a connection with the HIV virus; summarizing this view, the online *General Practice Notebook* states, "This term refers to a collection of sexually transmitted enteric infections in HIV infected homosexuals. The infective organisms include: Shigella, Giardia, Campylobacter-like organisms, Entamoeba, Chlamydia, gonorrhoea and syphilis" (see http://www.gpnotebook.co.uk/cache /-603586526.htm). Homosexual activists have exerted intense pressure on physicians to stop using the term, however, because it makes the link between cause and effect uncomfortably clear.